The proceeds from this book
will be donated to
The Kidderminster Railway Museum

THE RAILWAY
AT
KIDDERMINSTER
IN THE 1940s

Peter F. Curtis

0-6-0T 8727 in Kidderminster Yard in July 1947

A.J.TURLEY

First edition

Published 2005
By
Adrian & Neil Turley
1 Orchard Rise
Bewdley
Worcestershire DY12 2EW

ISBN 0-9537869-2-7

Printed by :
Veldonn Printers Ltd, Kidderminster
Worcestershire. Tel : 01562 68477

THE RAILWAY
AT
KIDDERMINSTER
IN THE 1940s

CONTENTS

INTRODUCTION AND ACKNOWLEDGEMENTS

During the 1940s the author lived near the railway and the Wooden Bridge. Many of his notes made during this period survive and make interesting reading. The purpose of this book is to put on record the large variety of locomotives that were to be seen at Kidderminster during that period, and to give some indication of the heavy traffic that came through.

Acknowledgements

Kidderminster Railway Museum
National Railway Museum, York
STEAM – Museum of the Great Western Railway, Swindon
English Heritage. NMR
Gloucestershire Record Office
U.S National Archives
Kidderminster Library
Kidderminster Shuttle
Simmons Aerofilms
Brintons Limited
The Historical Model Railway Society

A special thanks to Lyn Burns, the daughter of the late Peter Curtis, for permission to use his photographs in this book.

Robert Barber, Barry Cook, C.P Stacey/Initial Photographics, Roger Carpenter, Richard Casserley, Rex Conway, Steve Dockerty, Graham Gardner, Doris McKenzie-Keselowski, Alf Powick, Derek Plumb, Melvyn Thompson, Mike Webster, F.A Wycherley.

Photographic research by Neil Turley.

....

Some of the regular enthusiasts to be found on the Wooden Bridge during the war years :

Graham Barnbrook, Harry Brooks, John Buffrey, Ronald Crumpton, Peter Curtis, Albert Edwards, Keith Gordon, Stanford Jacobs, Brian Moone, Barry Penney, Bill Vaughan, Don Wilcox, Derek Yeomans, Roy Yeomans.

THE WOODEN BRIDGE

A. J. Turley

The favourite spot in Kidderminster to observe trains was the 'Wooden Bridge' which spanned the narrowest part of the goods yard south of the railway station. Although known locally as the 'Wooden Bridge' it was of steel construction with wooden decking over which was a pathway leading from the main Chester Road to Hoo Road. From this bridge one could see the Malvern Hills to the south and the wireless masts at Droitwich to the east.

Trains approaching from the south could be observed over a mile away, while those from the north could be seen as they came into the station. The goods yard was always very busy with the shunting engine working 24 hours a day with an additional engine during the sugar beet season.

During the wartime there were non railway interests which could be observed from the bridge. U.S Army convoys moving south along Chester Road in readiness for the D-Day invasion. If one went down the path to the roadway and shouted 'Any gum chum' there was always a possibility some goodies coming your way. Also on this road strange East Kent buses, including open top double deckers, could be seen taking workers to the I.C.I factory at Summerfield and to the 25MU RAF depot at Hartlebury. Also to be seen were the RAF 60 ft long "Queen Mary"s taking supplies to the depot. Between the bridge and the Chester Road to the left of the footpath was a brick built air raid shelter with a flat concrete roof.

In the coal yard just to the north of the footpath the Kidderminster Gas Company's Sentinel steam lorry (AW 7668) could be seen plying between the yard and the gasworks in the town.

The bridge was also an ideal spot for aeroplane spotting, All types of plane could be seen both British and American, and occasionally German! On one occasion the sky was full of what seemed to be hundreds of planes towing gliders. One gentleman could be found spending hours on the bridge not train spotting but aeroplane spotting, he did not seem to have any interest in the trains. We railway enthusiasts nicknamed him 'Aeroplane'.

The number taking boys on the bridge were generally tolerated despite being wartime, the one exception was a certain special constable who did not approve of our activities and cleared us off, but as soon as he was out of sight we were back! In the early part of the war an A.R.P Warden used to visit us to make sure we had our gas masks with us. Occasionally we were told off by a railway ganger for standing on the wire of the post and wire fencing in case we broke it, otherwise we were well behaved.

There was a field adjacent to the bridge, between the railway and a Shell Mex depot, where we could play cricket if there was a quiet period on the railway. If the ball was hit over the railway or the Shell Mex Depot it was six and out!

An American serviceman occasionally came on the bridge to watch the trains. The first time he saw one of the U.S.A S160 2-8-0s passing by on a goods train he remarked that in the States it would be used as a 'switch engine'

Train Spotting in 1940

In 1940 we did not have the benefit of the Ian Allan ABCs, these did not appear until later. We had to depend on the older enthusiasts who were members of either the Stephenson Locomotive Society or the Railway Correspondence and Travel Society to obtain details so that we could make our own reference books. This was quite a laborious job. The older lads showed us how to lay out these 'refs'. They insisted on a 'proper' procedure : The engine numbers were to be written in blue ink, the shed to which the engine was allocated was to be in pencil so that it could easily be altered if there was a change of depot. Space was then to be left for a 'PD' – the place and date where and when the engine was observed, this to be entered in red ink.

The young schoolboy spotters did not record which train the engine was working. However, a sample of 'cops' obtained in the early days are recorded here :

2 February 1940

4-6-0 'Hall'	5977 *Beckford Hall* (WOS)
2-8-0	2885 (BAN)
2-6-0 'Mogul'	5322 (OXY)
2-6-0 'Aberdare'	2679 (WOS)
0-6-0 'Dean'	2348 (SALOP), 2389 (STB), 2551 (WOS)
0-6-0 LNER Class J.25	2040 (WOS)
4-4-0 'Dukedog'	3208 (SRD)
2-8-0T	4257 (LTS)
2-6-2T	5110 (KDR), 5112 (KDR)
2-6-2T	4560 (WOS)
0-6-0T	8718 (KDR)

9 July 1940

4-6-0 'Hall'	5982 *Harrington Hall* (CARM), 5996 *Mytton Hall* (PDN), 5998 *Trevor Hall* (LA), 6900 *Abney Hall* (PDN)
4-6-0 'Grange'	6818 *Hardwick Grange* (NPT), 6842 *Nunhold Grange* (BL)
4-4-0 'Bulldog'	3379 *River Fal* (GLO)
4-4-0 'Dukedog'	3225 (ABH)
2-8-0 'ROD'	3048 (GLO)
2-8-0	2802 (PPRD), 2827 (PPRD)

2-8-0T	5219 (PFFN)
2-6-0 'Mogul'	6387 (WES), 7306 (NEY), 7311 (CHR)
0-6-0 'Collett'	2281 (STB)
0-6-0T	3702 (SALOP)

Halls 5996, 5998 and 6900 were brand new locomotives having been completed during June 1940. They were probably on the London trains.

When we were older we made notes recording which train an engine was seen on. This was a simple matter for passenger trains, but not easy for goods trains. Although there were regular goods turns they were not easily identifiable. In wartime they were liable to be heavily delayed, priority being given to military goods trains, troop trains and ambulance trains., sometimes waiting for hours on end on the goods loops at Kidderminster for a path. Relief engine crews would often arrive on a passenger train and walk from the station to take over.

A.J.Turley

Although not strictly a railway associated vehicle, this restored East Kent bus seen here at Bewdley in 2002, was one of several which had been drafted to the Kidderminster area during the war to transport workers to strategic sites in the district. These buses, including open top double deckers, could be seen from the Wooden Bridge passing along Chester Road.

7

KIDDERMINSTER STATION

R.S Carpenter

Kidderminster Station entrance.

R.K Blencoe

Kidderminster Station Signal Box

KIDDERMINSTER STATION

View looking towards Stourbridge.
The long excursion platform can be seen on the left.

View looking towards Worcester.

TICKETS ISSUED AT KIDDERMINSTER

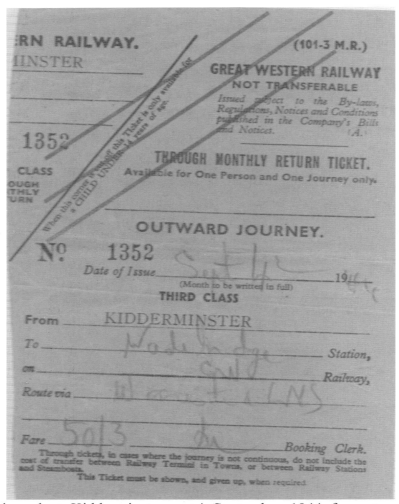

Paper ticket issued at Kidderminster on 4 September 1944 for outward journey to Wadebridge. Travel restrictions to costal areas in the West Country had only just been lifted.

Platform tickets issued at Kidderminster. The one on the left issued at the booking office, the other obtained from a platform ticket machine.

CHEAP DAY TICKETS RESTORED FROM 3 SEPTEMBER 1946

CHEAP DAY TICKETS

NOW ISSUED

at Single Fare for Double Journey to LARGE TOWNS and CITIES, on Tuesdays Wednesdays and Thursdays from Stations within a radius of approximately 20 miles

ALSO

CHEAP MARKET TICKETS

to MARKET TOWNS on certain weekdays from surrounding Stations

For further details and other reduced facilities
ENQUIRE AT YOUR LOCAL STATION

GWR

PADDINGTON STATION, LONDON, W.2

IMPROVED

WINTER FACILITIES NOW IN OPERATION

include

- More Main Line and Local Services
- More Restaurant and Buffet-Car Facilities
- Reservation of Seats on certain Long-Distance Expresses
- Restoration of many pre-war Cross Country Services

FOR ALL INFORMATION ENQUIRE AT YOUR LOCAL G.W.R STATION

PADDINGTON STATION, LONDON, W.2

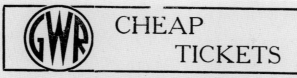

GWR CHEAP TICKETS

On TUESDAYS, WEDNESDAYS and THURSDAYS

commencing

SEPTEMBER 3rd

Cheap Day Tickets

WILL BE ISSUED FROM THE UNDERMENTIONED STATIONS TO

KIDDERMINSTER

FROM					Return Fare, Third Class	
					s.	d.
BIRMINGHAM (Snow Hill)					3	4
Handsworth (G.W.)					2	11
Smethwick Junction					2	8
Oldbury and Langley Green	..	..	..	..	2	5
Rowley Regis and Blackheath					2	3
Old Hill					2	0
Cradley Heath and Cradley					1	9
Lye					1	7
STOURBRIDGE JUNCTION					1	3
STOURBRIDGE TOWN					1	4
Brettell Lane	..	..			1	8
Brierley Hill					1	9
Blowers Green	..				2	1
Dudley					2	4
Bilston W.M.					2	9
Priestfield					3	0
WOLVERHAMPTON (Low Level)					3	4

Children under Three years of age, Free. Three and under Fourteen years Half-fare.

NOTICE AS TO CONDITIONS.—Tickets are available for day of issue only by any train in each direction and are not transferable. Break of journey not allowed.

These tickets are issued subject to the conditions of issue of ordinary passenger tickets where applicable and also to the special conditions as set out in the Ticket, etc., Regulations, By-Laws and General Notices.

Luggage allowances are as set out in these General Notices.

TICKETS ISSUED AND DATED IN ADVANCE AT STATIONS AND OFFICES.

Any further information may be obtained from :
Mr. A. V. R. BROWN, Divisional Superintendent, Snow Hill Station, Birmingham. *Telephone Central 5071 (extension "Enquiries")*; or from
Mr. GILBERT MATTHEWS, Superintendent of the Line, Paddington Station, W.2. *Telephone Paddington 7000 (extension "Enquiries," 8.0 a.m to 10.0 p.m.).*

Paddington Station, August, 1946.   JAMES MILNE, General Manager.

B.11 31 40. B.H. 10,000.   Printed in Great Britain by Joseph Wones, Ltd., West Bromwich: also Birmingham and London.

LOCAL TICKETS

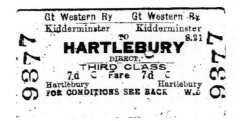
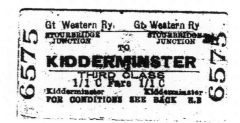

Kidderminster to Hartlebury Single   Stourbridge Junction to Kidderminster Single

Kidderminster to Hartlebury Monthly Return

Foley Park Halt to Bewdley Monthly Return. This is a ticket that would have been issued by the guard on the Auto Train.

Kidderminster to Worcester Child Cheap Day Return. Child tickets were cut diagonally in half where no specially printed child tickets were available.

Kidderminster to Lye Workman's Return. Workman's tickets were grey in colour instead of the green and issued before 8.0 a.m.

Return half of Child Cheap Day Return Kidderminster to Wolverhampton.

THE GOODS YARDS

National Railway Museum

Electric crane at Kidderminster Goods Depot
Sentinel Steam Lorry belonging to Steel Stampings, Cookley in background.
The Gas Company had a similar Sentinel for conveying coke to the gasworks during the
1940s.

The goods yard was extremely busy. Shunting being in operation continuously from
6.0 am on Monday morning until 2.0 pm on Sunday.

Goods handled included :
    Traffic from the Severn Valley and Tenbury lines.
    Sugar beet, limestone and coal for the British Sugar Corporation at Foley Park.
    Molasses and refined sugar from the British Sugar Corporation.
    Jute from Dundee for the local carpet factories.
    Grain for Messrs Harvey & Co.
    Coke for the local gasworks.
    Sand for use in foundries from quarries in the area.
    Carpets.
    Coal for the local coal merchants.

THE GOODS YARD

Aerial view of the railway at Kidderminster in 1938 showing the layout of the goods yard
prior to the wartime extensions.

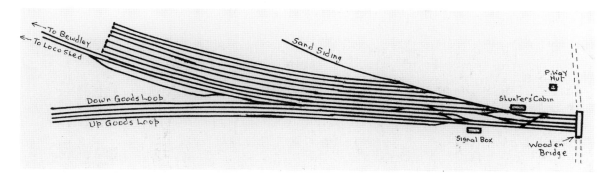

1940 LAYOUT OF BOTTOM YARD

The bottom yard was enlarged in 1943. Three additional marshalling yard sidings and two sidings for Wagon Repairs Ltd. were added. The old Shunters' Cabin was demolished and a new one constructed near to the Wooden Bridge. To enable the contractor's (Tarslag Ltd) equipment to access the site the public footpath was bulldozed near the Permanent Way hut and a temporary wooden bridge was built to enable pedestrians to reach Aggborough from the Chester Road.

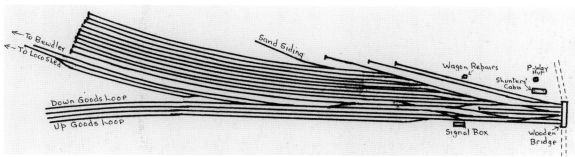

1944 LAYOUT OF BOTTOM YARD

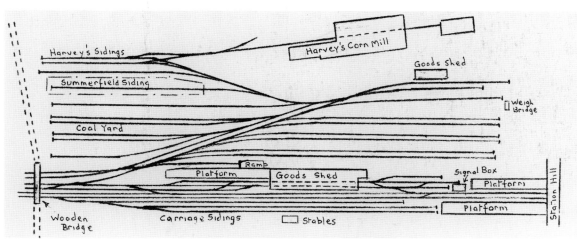

1944 LAYOUT OF TOP YARD

15

Kidderminster Goods Yard (contd)

The Summerfield Siding, which was enclosed by a security fence, together with an adjoining siding were added at the same time as the extensions to the bottom yard. The coal yard sidings were also slightly re-aligned.

Kidderminster Library

Aerial view of the Top Yard

Kidderminster Railway Museum / Geoff Bannister Collection

Top Yard viewed from Station Approach.

THE RAILWAYMEN

Nearly 300 railwaymen were employed at Kidderminster in the 1940s. The following is a list compiled with the help of Graham Gardner, an ex railway employee, of the various posts.

Goods Depot
- Goods Agent
- Chief Clerk
- 5 Senior Clerks
- 25 Goods Inwards Outwards Clerks
- 2 Loading Deck Foremen
- Approx 20 Loading Deck Porters
- 1 Road Crane Driver
- 2 Slingers
- 1 Wagon Number Taker
- Weighbridge Attendant
- Motor Depot Foreman
- 5 Mechanics
- Road Transport Drivers

Goods Yard
- 2 Yard Foremen
- 9 Shunters
- 2 Wagon Examiners
- 4 Wagon Repairers
- 8 Yard Men
- 1 Stable Man

Passenger Station
- Station Master
- Station Master's Clerk
- Station Inspector
- Chief Booking Clerk
- 2 Booking Clerks
- Switchboard Operator
- Refreshment Room Staff
- Office Cleaner
- 2 Ticket Collectors
- 4 Porters
- 1 Junior Porter
- Senior Parcels Clerk
- Junior Parcels Clerk
- 2 Senior Parcels Porters
- 4 Parcels Porters
- 2 Parcels Van Drivers

Locomotive Depot
- Shed Foreman
- Approx 25 sets Footplate Men
- (Drivers and Firemen)
- 4 Fitters
- 8 Cleaners
- 1 Boiler Man
- 4 Shed Men
- 1 Clerk

Traffic Department / P-Way / S &T
- 8 Passenger Guards
- 2 Passenger Shunters
- 6 Goods Guards
- 6 Signalmen
- 1 Lamp Man
- 8 Gangers

5.40 a.m   Foley Park Halt, Bewdley, Arley, Highley
5.50 a.m   All stations to Birmingham S.H
6.15 a.m   All stations to Birmingham
6.50 a.m   Foley Park Halt, Bewdley, Arley, Highley
6.50 a.m   All stations to Wolverhampton
7.7 a.m   Hagley, Stourbridge Junc. Cradley Heath and stations to Birmingham S.H.
7.10 a.m   Bewdley
7.14 a.m   Hartlebury, Droitwich, Worcester F.S and Henwick.
7.23 a.m   All stations to Birmingham S.H.
7.39 a.m   Foley Park Halt and Bewdley
7.43 a.m   Churchill & Blakedown, Hagley, Stourbridge Junc., Lye, Cradley Heath, Old Hill, Smethwick Junc., Handsworth & Smethwick and Birmingham S.H.
8..0 a.m   Hagley, Stourbridge Junc., Lye, Cradley Heath, Old Hill, Rowley Regis & Blackheath and Birmingham S.H.
8.9 a.m   Stations to Worcester S.H., Evesham, Honeybourne, Moreton-in-Marsh, Oxford, Reading and London Paddington.
8.14 a.m   Foley Park Halt and Bewdley
8.19 a.m   Stourbridge Junc., Oldbury & Langley Green and Birmingham S.H.
8.24 a.m   All stations to Birmingham S.H.
8.35 a.m   Worcester F.S., Gt. Malvern, Hereford, Pontrilas, Abergavenny, Pontypool Rd., Newport and Cardiff.
9.20 a.m   Hagley, Stourbridge Junc., Old Hill, Rowley Regis & Blackheath, Oldbury &Langley Green, Smethwick Junc. and Birmingham S.H.
9.33 a.m   All stations to Oxford
10.2 a.m   Stations to Wolverhampton, Wellington, Market Drayton and Crewe.
10.10 a.m   All stations to Birmingham S.H.
10.16 a.m   Bewdley and stations to Woofferton
10.40 a.m   Bewdley and stations to Shrewsbury
11.10 a.m   Droitwich Spa, Worcester F.S., Malvern Link, Great Malvern, Malvern Wells, Colwall, Ledbury and Hereford.
11.16 a.m   Stourbridge Junc. and Birmingham S.H.
11.28 a.m   Stations to Worcester S.H.
12.10 p.m (S.O) Stourbridge Junc., and stations to Birmingham S.H.
12.40 p.m (S.O) Stations to Highley.
12.45 p.m   Stourbridge Junc., Smethwick Junc. and Birmingham S.H.
1.25 p.m   Hartlebury, Droitwich Spa, Worcester S.H, Evesham, Moreton-in-Marsh, Oxford, Reading and London Paddington.
1.30 p.m (SX) Foley Park Halt and Bewdley.
1.30 p.m   All stations to Birmingham S.H. except Soho & Winson Green and Hockley
1.39 p.m   Droitwich Spa, Worcester F.S, Malvern Link, Great Malvern, Colwall, Ledbury, Hereford, Abergavenny, Pontypool Road, Newport and Cardiff.
1.50 p.m   Bewdley and stations to Woofferton
1.54 p.m   All stations to Wolverhampton
2.24 p.m (S.O) All stations to Birmingham S.H.
2.48 p.m   All stations to Ledbury
3.3 p.m   Hartlebury, Droitwich Spa, Fernhill Heath, Worcester S.H and principal stations to London Paddington.
3.15 p.m   All stations to Birmingham S.H.
3.25 p.m   Hartlebury
3.45 p.m   Bewdley and stations to Bridgnorth.
4.4 p.m   Stations to Worcester S.H.
4.16 p.m   Stourbridge Junc., Smethwick Junc. and Birmingham S.H.

4.20 p.m   Foley Park Halt, Bewdley,, Burlish Hlt, Stourport-on-Severn and Hartlebury.
4.25 p.m   All stations to Birmingham S.H.
4.30 p.m   Droitwich Spa, Worcester F.S, Malvern Link and Great Malvern
4.38 p.m   Bewdley and all stations to Woofferton
5.0 p.m   Hartlebury, Droitwich Spa, Worcester S.H.
5.41 p.m   Worcester F.S, Malvern Link, Great Malvern, Malvern Wells, Colwall, Ledbury, Hereford and stations to Cardiff.
5.42 p.m   Stourbridge Junc. and Birmingham S.H.
5.48 p.m   All stations to Woofferton
5.56 p.m   Churchill & Blakedown, Hagley and Stourbridge Junc.
5.59 p.m   All stations to Worcester S.H
6.20 p.m   All stations to Birmingham S.H.
6.34 p.m   Hartlebury, Droitwich Spa, Worcester F.S, Malvern Link, Great Malvern and Malvern Wells.
6.40 p.m   Foley Park Halt, Bewdley, Burlish Halt, Stourport-on-Severn and Hartlebury.
7.0 p.m   All stations to Wolverhampton
7.32 p.m   Hartlebury, Droitwich Spa, Fernhill Heath and Worcester F.S.
7.57 p.m   Hartlebury, Droitwich Spa and Worcester F.S.
8.6 p.m   Stourbridge Junc., Old Hill, Rowley Regis &Blackheath, Smethwick Junc and Birmingham S.H.
8.15 p.m   Foley Park Halt, Bewdley and stations to Bridgnorth.
8.27 p.m   Churchill & Blakedown, Hagley and Stourbridge Junc.
8.53 p.m   Stourbridge Junc.
9.13 p.m   Droitwich Spa, Worcester F.S, Malvern Link, Great Malvern, Colwall, Ledbury and Hereford
9.28 p.m   Hartlebury, Droitwich Spa and Worcester S.H.
10.4 p.m   All stations to Birmingham S.H.

SUNDAYS

9.8 a.m   Bewdley and Stourport-on-Severn
9.50 a.m   Hartlebury, Droitwich Spa Fernhill Heath, Worcester S.H and principal stations to London Paddington.
10.18 a.m   All stations to Birmingham S.H.
10.47 a.m   Stourbridge Junc., Smethwick Junc. and Birmingham S.H.
11.26 a.m   Stations to Wolverhampton.
12.41 p.m   Worcester F.S, Great Malvern and Hereford.
2.43 p.m   Stations to Wolverhampton
3.57 p.m   Hartlebury.
4.16 p.m   Stourbridge Junc. and Birmingham S.H.
5.26 p.m   Hartlebury, Droitwich Spa, Fernhill Heath and Worcester S.H.
5.44 p.m   Droitwich Spa, Worcester F.S and principal stations to Cardiff.
6.57 p.m   All stations to Birmingham S.H
8.24 p.m   Hartlebury, Droitwich Spa, Worcester F.S, Henwick, Malvern Link and Great Malvern.
8.49 p.m   Stations to Wolverhampton.
9.29 p.m   Hartlebury, Droitwich Spa and Worcester S.H.
10.17 p.m   Stourbridge Junc. and stations to Birmingham S.H.

Passenger train departures from Kidderminster   June 1947

5.45 a.m   All stations to Birmingham S.H.

5.53 a.m   Foley Park Halt, Bewdley, Arley and Highley.

6.14 a.m   All stations to Birmingham S.H except Soho & Winson Green.

6.48 a.m   All stations to Wolverhampton.

7.0 a.m   Foley Park Halt and Bewdley.

7.5 a.m (SX)   Hartlebury.

7.10 a.m   All stations to Birmingham S.H.

7.22 a.m   Hartlebury, Droitwich Spa, Fernhill Heath, Worcester F.S and Henwick.

7.32 a.m   All stations to Wolverhampton.

7.39 a.m   Foley Park Halt and Bewdley.

7.43 a.m   Churchill & Blakedown, Hagley, Stourbridge Junc., Lye, Cradley Heath, Old Hill, Smethwick Junc., Handsworth & Smethwick and Birmingham S.H.

8.0 a.m   Hagley, Stourbridge Junc.Lye, Cradley, Old Hill, Rowley Regis & Blackheath and Birmingham S.H.

8.2 a.m   Stations to Worcester S.H, Evesham, Moreton-in-Marsh, Oxford and London Paddington.

8.19 a.m   Stourbridge Junc.,Oldbury & Langley Green, Smethwick Junc. and Birmingham S.H.

8.24 a.m   All stations to Birmingham S.H.

8.35 a.m   Worcester F.S, Great Malvern, Hereford, Abergavenny, Pontypool Rd, Newport and Cardiff.

8.50 a.m   All stations to Woofferton.

8.53 a.m   Stourbridge Junc.,Smethwick Junc. and Birmingham S.H.

8.55 a.m (SX) All stations to Worcester F.S.

9.25 a.m   Hagley, Stourbridge Junc.,Old Hill, Rowley Regis & Blackheath, Oldbury & Langley Green, Smethwick Junc and Birmingham S.H.

9.33 a.m   All stations to Oxford.

10.8 a.m   Stations to Wolverhampton,, Wellington, Market Drayton and Crewe.

10.18 a.m   All stations to Woofferton.

10.27 a.m (SO) Droitwich Spa, Worcester F.S and principal stations to Cardiff.

10.28 a.m   All stations to Birmingham S.H.

10.35 am   Foley Park Halt, Bewdley and all stations to Shrewsbury.

11.28 a.m   Stourbridge Junc. and Birmingham S.H.

11.29 a.m   Stations to Worcester S.H.

11.58 a.m   Hartlebury, Droitwich Spa, Worcester F.S, Malvern Link, Great Malvern,, Colwall, Ledbury and Hereford.

12.40 p.m (SO) All stations to Highley.

12.53 p.m   Stourbridge Junc., Smethwick Junc. and Birmingham S.H.

1.25 p.m   Hartlebury, Droitwich Spa, Worcester S.H and principal stations to London Paddington

1.30 p.m   All stations to Birmingham S.H.

1.31 p.m (SO) 1.45 p.m(SX) Foley Park Halt and Bewdley.

1.39 p.m   Droitwich Spa, Worcester F.S, and principal stations to Cardiff.

1.54 p.m   All stations to Wolverhampton

2.10 p.m   All stations to Woofferton.

3.2 p.m   All stations to Worcester S.H, Pershore, Evesham, Honeybourne, Moreton-in-Marsh, Kingham and Oxford.

3.25 p.m   Hartlebury

3.30 p.m   All stations to Bridgnorth.

4.30 p.m   Droitwich Spa, Worcester F.S, Malvern Link, Great Malvern, Malvern Wells, Colwall, Ledbury and Hereford.

4.36 p.m   Stourbridge Junc.,Smethwick Junc and Birmingham S.H.

4.38 p.m   All stations to Woofferton.

4.48 p.m   All stations to Birmingham S.H.

5.0 p.m   All stations to Worcester S.H.
5.24 p.m   Churchill & Blakedown, Hagley and Stourbridge Junc.
5.36 p.m   Churchill & Blakedown, Hagley and Stourbridge Junc,
5.42 p.m   Droitwich Spa, Worcester F.S, and principal stations to Cardiff.
5.48 p.m   All stations to Highley
5.55 p.m   Stourbridge Junc. and Birmingham S.H.
5.58 p.m   All stations to Worcester S.H.
6.19 p.m   Droitwich Spa, Worcester F.S, Malvern Link, Great Malvern and Malvern Wells.
6.20 p.m   All stations to Birmingham S.H.
6.25 p.m   All stations to Woofferton.
7.8 p.m   All stations to Wolverhampton.
7.57 p.m   Hartlebury, Droitwich Spa, Fernhill Heath and Worcester.S.H.
8.10 p.m   Foley Park Halt, Bewdley, Burlish Halt, Stourport-on-Severn, Hartlebury, Droitwich Spa and Worcester S.H.
8.13 p.m   All stations to Wolverhampton.
8.36 p.m(SO) Stourbridge Junc., Smethwick Junc and Birmingham S.H.
8.57 p.m   Droitwich Spa, Worcester F.S, Malvern Link, Great Malvern, Colwall, Ledbury and Hereford.
9.5 p.m   All stations to Birmingham S.H.
9.28 p.m   Hartlebury, Droitwich Spa and Worcester S.H.
10.8 p.m   All stations to Birmingham S.H.

SUNDAYS

7.45 a.m   All stations to Birmingham S.H.
8.34 a.m   Bewdley and all stations to Bridgnorth.
9.8 a.m   Bewdley and Stourport-on-Severn.
9.37 a.m   Hartlebury, Droitwich Spa, Fernhill Heath, Worcester S.H and stations to Oxford.
10.34 a.m All stations to Birmingham S.H.
11.10 a.m Stourbridge Junc., Smethwick Junc and Birmingham S.H.
11.25 a.m Churchill & Blakedown, Hagley, Stourbridge Junc. and stations to Wolverhampton.
12.35 p.m Worcester F.S, Great Malvern and Hereford.
2.22 p.m   Churchill & Blakedown, Hagley, Stourbridge Junc. and stations to Wolverhampton.
3.54 p.m   Hartlebury.
4.21 p.m   Stourbridge Junc. and Birmingham S.H.
5.8 p.m   Hartlebury, Droitwich Spa, Fernhill Heath and Worcester S.H.
5.32 p.m   Droitwich Spa, Worcester F.S and principal stations to Cardiff.
6.42 p.m   All stations to Birmingham S.H.
7.50 p.m   Stourbridge Junc. and all stations to Birmingham S.H.
8.55 p.m   Churchill & Blakedown, Hagley, Stourbridge Junc. and stations to Wolverhampton.
9.20 p.m   All stations to Birmingham S.H.
9.28 p.m   Hartlebury, Droitwich Spa and Worcester S.H.

PASSENGER SERVICES
Wolverhampton to Paddington via West Midland Line

Trains for Paddington called at Kidderminster on weekdays at 8.2 am, 1.25 pm. On Sundays at 9.37 am.   Additionally there was a train to Oxford on weekdays at 9.33 am.

Trains from Paddington called at Kidderminster on weekdays at 1.54 pm, 5.36 pm and 8.13 pm. On Sundays at 8.55 pm.

These trains produced a wide variety of named locomotives.

6.50 am Wolverhampton to Paddington
8.2 am Kidderminster

31 May 1945	4101 (SRD)	7 August 1948	1016 *County of Hants* (SRD)
2 April 1945	5021 *Whittington Castle* (SRD)	2 Oct 1948	1017 *County of Hereford* (SRD)
23 May 1945	5053 *Earl Cairns* (SRD)	9 Oct 1948	5088 *Llanthony Abbey* (SRD)
2 June 1945	5967 *Bickmarsh Hall* (BAN)	6 Nov 1948	4000 *North Star* (SRD)
5 Aug 1946	7315 (SRD)	13 Nov 1948	1025 *County of Radnor* (SRD)
7 March 1947	5038 *Morlais Castle* (PDN)	17 Nov 1948	5022 *Wigmore Castle* (SRD)
7 April 1947	4061 *Glastonbury Abbey* (SRD)	20 Nov 1948	1017 *County of Hereford* (SRD)
26 May 1947	7007 *Ogmore Castle* (SRD)	27 Nov 1948	1025 *County of Radnor* (SRD)
18 May 1948	1029 *County of Worcester (SRD)*	4 Dec 1948	5075 *Wellington* (SRD)
31 July 1948	6321 (SRD)	8 Jan 1949	5053 *Earl Cairns* (SRD)
2 Aug 1948	2981 *Ivanhoe* (BAN)	26 Feb 1949	1024 *County of Pembroke* (SRD)
3 Aug 1948	2930 *Saint Vincent* (CHR)		

The locomotive on this service returned to Wolverhampton on the 9.35 am Worcester S.H to Crewe passenger. (Kidderminster 10.8 am)

12.5 pm Wolverhampton to Paddington
1.25 pm Kidderminster

2 April 1945	4014 *Knight of the Bath* (SRD)	8 Mar 1947	5063 *Earl Baldwin* (WOS)
14 April 1945	5036 *Lyonshall Castle* (PDN)	24 May 1947	7007 *Ogmore Castle* (PDN)
21 April 1945	6970 un-named (OXY)	26 May 1947	4046 *Princess Mary* (SALOP)
28 April 1945	5027 *Farleigh Castle* (PDN)	15 May 1948	1029 *County of Worcester* (SRD)
21 May 1945	5968 *Cory Hall* (WEY)	17 May 1948	6970 *Whaddon Hall* (OXY)
22 May 1945	6964 un-named (SRD)	19 May 1948	6842 *Nunhold Grange* (SPM)
2 June 1945	4033 *Queen Victoria* (BL)	24 July 1948	5995 *Wick Hall* (SRD)
16 June 1945	4903 *Astley Hall* (OXF)	31 July 1948	4961 *Pyrland Hall* (PDN)
30 June 1945	4059 *Princess Patricia* (GLO)	2 Aug 1948	4061 *Glastonbury Abbey* (SALOP)
7 July 1945	4982 *Acton Hall* (LDR)	3 Aug 1948	4046 *Princess Mary* (SALOP)
23 March 1946	4021 *British Monarch* (OXF)	14 Aug 1948	5958 *Knolton Hall* (CDF)
30 March 1946	4052 *Princess Beatrice* (OXF)	2 Oct 1948	1029 *County of Worcester* (SRD)
6 April 1946	4090 *Dorchester Castle* (LA)	9 Oct 1948	1017 *County of Hereford* (SRD)
13 April 1946	4025 un-named (SRD)	13 Nov 1948	5015 *Kingswear Castle* (SRD)
20 April 1946	4013 *Knight of St. Patrick* (SRD)	28 Dec 1948	4060 *Princess Eugenie* (SRD)
27 April 1946	5035 *Coity Castle* (PDN)	1 Jan 1949	4018 *Knight of the Grand Cross* (SRD)
25 May 1946	4004 *Morning Star (OXF)*	8 Jan 1949	5015 *Kingswear Castle* (SRD)
1 June 1946	6875 *Hindford Grange* (PPRD)	18 April 1949	5053 *Earl Cairns (SRD)*
5 Aug 1946	5045 *Earl of Dudley* (PDN)	6 Nov 1949	1025 *County of Radnor* (SRD)
1 Mar 1947	1017 *County of Hereford* (SRD)		

PASSENGER SERVICES

8.00 am Wolverhampton to Paddington (Sundays)
9.37 am Kidderminster

In December 1940 Wolverhampton Stafford Road shed acquired two 47xx 2-8-0 locomotives 4704 and 4708. These were frequently used on the Sunday morning service to Paddington via the West Midland line.

This was a most unusual type to be seen at Kidderminster, in addition to 4704 and 4708. 4701 (PDN) was also noted on this train on 31 May 1942. No other examples of this class have ever been recorded at Kidderminster.

A.Norman H. Glover

4708 at Oxley shed   1 July 1939

Other observations on this service :

8 July 1945	4033 *Queen Victoria* (BL)	7 Nov 1948	6859 *Yiewsley Grange* (CHR)
2 March 1947	5022 *Wigmore Castle* (PDN)	14 Nov 1948	1017 *County of Hereford* (SRD)
9 March 1947	5063 *Earl Baldwin* (WOS)	9 Jan 1949	4018 *Knight of the Grand Cross* (SRD)
29 June 1947	4000 *North Star* (SRD)	16 Jan 1949	7010 *Avondale Castle* (OXF)
14 Jan 1948	1017 *County of Hereford* (SRD	23 Jan 1949	4018 *Knight of the Grand Cross* (SRD)
11 July 1948	6923 *Croxteth Hall* (DID)	13 Feb 1949	1024 *County of Pembroke* (SRD)
25 July 1948	1017 *County of Hereford* (SRD	20 Feb 1949	5022 *Wigmore Castle* (SRD)
8 Aug 1948	7008 *Swansea Castle* (OXF)	27 Feb 1949	5942 *Doldowlod Hall* (SRD)
15 Aug 1948	7008 *Swansea Castle* (OXF)	6 Mar 1949	1025 *County of Radnor* (SRD)
26 Sept 1948	4053 *Princess Alexandra* (SRD	20 Mar 1949	5088 *Llanthony Abbey* (SRD)
3 Oct 1948	4938 *Liddington Hall* (OXF)	27 Mar 1949	5995 *Wick Hall* (SRD)
10 Oct 1948	1017 *County of Hereford* (SRD	24 July 1949	6851 *Hurst Grange* (WOS)

PASSENGER SERVICES

8.18 am Wolverhampton to Oxford
9.33 am Kidderminster

23 May 1945	5065 *Newport Castle* (PDN)	2 Oct 1948	7010 *Avondale Castle* (OXF)
5 August 1946	5075 *Wellington* (SRD)	9 Oct 1948	7010 *Avondale Castle* (OXF)
7 April 1947	1016 *County of Hants* (SRD)	6 Nov 1948	7008 *Swansea Castle* (OXF)
24 May 1947	5018 *St. Mawes Castle* (SRD)	22 Jan 1949	5040 *Stokesay Castle* (PDN)
26 May 1947	5018 *St. Mawes Castle* (SRD)	5 Feb 1949	4900 *Saint Martin* (PDN)
15 May 1948	1016 *County of Hants* (SRD)	12 Feb 1949	7008 *Swansea Castle* (OXF)
19 June 1948	7008 *Swansea Castle* (OXF)	19 Feb 1949	7008 *Swansea Castle* (OXF)
3 July 1948	7010 *Avondale Castle* (OXF)	26 Feb 1949	7010 *Avondale Castle* (OXF)
2 August 1948	5018 *St. Mawes Castle* (SRD	5 March 1949	7010 *Avondale Castle* (OXF)
3 August 1948	7008 *Swansea Castle* (OXF)	12 March 1949	7010 *Avondale Castle* (OXF)
7 August 1948	6827 *Llanfrechfra Grange* (CDF)	18 April 1949	1016 *County of Hants* (SRD)
14 August 1948	6906 *Chicheley Hall* (BAN)	19 April 1949	6906 *Chicheley Hall* (BAN)
8 June 1949	6929 *Whorlton Hall* (BAN)	23 July 1949	4999 *Gopsal Hall* (TYS)
13 August 1949	6846 *Ruckley Grange* (SPM)	17 Sept 1949	5006 *Tregenna Castle* (CDF)
24 Sept 1949	1007 *County of Brecknock* (BL)	15 Oct 1949	4043 *Prince Henry* (BL)
22 Oct 1949	4034 *Queen Adelaide* (BL)	5 Nov 1949	4062 *Malmesbury Abbey* (SDN)
26 Nov 1949	4902 *Aldenham Hall* (OXF)	24 Dec 1949	4960 *Pyle Hall* (SRD)

7008 *Swansea Castle* and 7010 *Avondale Castle* , built Swindon May / June 1948 were painted in an experimental light green livery.

Peter F.Curtis

1016 *County of Hants* on 9.33 am to Oxford July 1947

PASSENGER SERVICES

9.45 am Paddington to Wolverhampton
1.54 pm Kidderminster

14 Nov 1947	5039 *Rhuddlan Castle* (PDN) *	19 Feb 1949	6964 *Thornbridge Hall* (SRD)
6 Mar 1948	4961 *Pyrland Hall* (PDN)	26 Feb 1949	5070 *Sir Daniel Gooch* (SRD)
10 July 1948	7013 *Bristol Castle* (PDN)	5 Mar 1949	5014 *Goodrich Castle* (PDN)
24 July 1948	4985 *Allesley Hall* (PDN)	12 Mar 1949	7004 *Eastnor Castle* (PDN)
31 July 1948	7013 *Bristol Castle* (PDN)	19 Mar 1949	6959 *Peatling Hall* (PDN)
2 Aug 1948	7013 *Bristol Castle* (PDN)	24 Mar 1949	1010 *County of Carnarvon* (PDN)
3 Aug 1948	7013 *Bristol Castle* (PDN)	25 Mar 1949	7001 *Sir James Milne* (PDN)
7 Aug 1948	6919 *Tylney Hall* (CARM)	26 Mar 1949	6961 *Stedham Hall* (SHL)
18 Aug 1948	6961 *Stedham Hall* (PDN)	28 Mar 1949	6981 *Marbury Hall* (BL)
25 Sept 1948	6855 *Saighton Grange* (WES)	29 Mar 1949	4992 *Crosby Hall* (SPM)
2 Oct 1948	5987 *Brocket Hall* (PDN)	2 April 1949	7013 *Bristol Castle* (PDN)
9 Oct 1948	6961 *Stedham Hall* (PDN)	9 April 1949	1021 *County of Montgomery* (PDN)
16 Oct 1948	5987 *Brocket Hall* (PDN)	16 April 1949	7013 *Bristol Castle* (PDN)
6 Nov 1948	7007 *Great Western* (PDN)	18 April 1949	1021 *County of Montgomery* (PDN)
13 Nov 1948	5065 *Upton Castle* (PDN)	1 May 1949	1000 *County of Middlesex* (PDN)
20 Nov 1948	1026 *County of Salop* (PDN)	7 May 1949	1008 *County of Cardigan* (PDN)
27 Nov 1948	5004 *Llanstephan Castle* (PDN)	14 May 1949	7007 *Great Western* (PDN)
4 Dec 1948	1026 *County of Salop* (PDN)	21 May 1949	5015 *Kingswear Castle* (SRD)
11 Dec 1948	5040 *Stokesay Castle* (PDN)	28 May 1949	5900 *Hinderton Hall* (WES)
18 Dec 1948	1026 *County of Salop* (PDN)	4 June 1949	6856 *Stowe Grange* (OXY)
24 Dec 1948	6929 *Whorlton Hall* (BAN)	6 June 1949	1015 *County of Gloucester* (PDN)
28 Dec 1948	6973 *Bricklehampton Hall* (PDN)	18 June 1949	6959 *Peatling Hall* (PDN)
11 Jan 1949	7007 *Great Western* (PDN)	25 June 1949	6869 *Resolven Grange* (PDN)
8 Jan 1949	1026 *County of Salop* (PDN)	7 July 1949	5987 *Brocket Hall* (PDN)
22 Jan 1949	4900 *Saint Martin* (PDN)	13 Aug 1949	5996 *Mytton Hall* (PDN)
29 Jan 1949	5066 *Wardour Castle* (PDN)	20 Aug 1949	6810 *Blakemere Grange* (LLY)

* 5039 was an oil burner

OIL BURNERS

Due to the coal shortage in 1946/47 a number of passenger and freight locomotives were converted to oil burning.

The only regular service through Kidderminster with oil burning locomotives was the 9.45 am Paddington to Wolverhampton and its return working the 3.45 pm Wolverhampton to Worcester.

5039 *Rhuddlan Castle* was one of 5 Castles to be converted in December 1946.

The scheme was, however, short lived the locomotives were altered back to coal burning by September 1948.

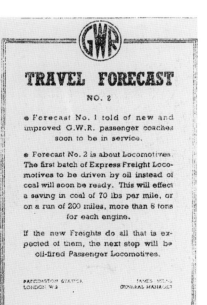

TRAVEL FORECAST
NO. 2

● Forecast No. 1 told of new and improved G.W.R. passenger coaches soon to be in service.

● Forecast No. 2 is about Locomotives. The first batch of Express Freight Locomotives to be driven by oil instead of coal will soon be ready. This will effect a saving in coal of 70 lbs per mile, or on a run of 200 miles, more than 6 tons for each engine.

If the new Freights do all that is expected of them, the next step will be oil-fired Passenger Locomotives.

PADDINGTON STATION, LONDON W.2   JAMES MILNE, GENERAL MANAGER

PASSENGER SERVICES

7.10 am Cardiff to Birmingham S.H. (Sundays)
Kidderminster 11.10 am

18 March 1945	5064 *Bishop's Castle* (SALOP)	6 June 1948	5005 *Manorbier Castle* (CDF)
25 March 1945	5086 *Viscount Horne* (SALOP)	13 June 1948	5007 *Rougemont Castle* (CDF)
1 April 1945	5064 *Bishop's Castle* (SALOP)	20 June 1948	5020 *Trematon Castle* (CDF)
8 April 1945	5015 *Kingswear Castle* (SALOP)	27 June 1948	7006 *Lydford Castle* (CDF)
29 April 1945	5064 *Bishop's Castle* (SALOP)	4 July 1948	5007 *Rougemont Castle* (CDF)
6 May 1945	5064 *Bishop's Castle* (SALOP)	11 July 1948	5995 *Wick Hall* (SRD)
13 May 1945	5046 *Earl Cawdor* (SALOP)	18 July 1948	5922 *Caxton Hall* (PDN)
24 June 1945	5097 *Sarum Castle* (SALOP)	25 July 1948	5065 *Newport Castle* (PDN)
19 August 1945	4035 *Queen Charlotte* (BL)	1 August 1948	4079 *Pendennis Castle* (HFD)
13 Oct 1946	1005 *County of Devon* (BL) **	8 August 1948	5964 *Wolseley Hall* (SPM)
20 Oct 1946	7006 *Lydford Castle* (SALOP)	15 August 1948	6866 *Morfa Grange* (TYS)
8 Dec 1946	5073 *Blenheim* (SALOP	5 Sept 1948	4979 *Wootton Hall* (CDF)
2 March 1947	5097 *Sarum Castle* (SALOP)	19 Sept 1948	5900 *Hinderton Hall* (WES)
9 March 1947	5030 *Shirburn Castle* (CDF)	26 Sept 1948	5900 *Hinderton Hall* (WES)
1 June 1947	4033 *Queen Victoria* (BL)	3 Oct 1948	2920 *Saint David* (HFD)
29 June 1947	5086 *Viscount Horne* (SALOP)		

** First County to be noted at Kidderminster

From the commencement of the 1948 winter timetable this train was worked by Pontypool Road, the same loco rostered for weeks on end.

6805 *Broughton Grange* (PPRD) 10 October 1948 until 20 February 1949

4912 *Berrington Hall* (PPRD)   27 February 1949 until 8 May 1949

With the commencement of the summer timetable a wider variety of locomotives were to be seen.

29 May 1949	6932 *Burwarton Hall* (PDN)	5 June 1949	6986 *Roydon Hall* ((SPM)
12 June 1949	5949 *Trematon Hall* (SPM)	19 June 1949	7811 *Dunley Manor* (BAN)
10 July 1949	5994 *Roydon Hall* (SALOP)	17 July 1949	4917 *Crosswood Hall* (TYS)
7 August 1949	5946 *Marwell Hall* (CDF)	14 August 1949	6939 *Calveley Hall* (CDF)
21 August 1949	4055 *Princess Sophia* (SDN)	28 August 1949	4904 *Binnegar Hall* (OXY)
25 Sept 1949	5984 *Linden Hall* (BL)		

From the commencement of the 1949 winter timetable this train was again worked by Pontypool Road shed, the same locomotive rostered each week.

5975 *Winslow Hall* (PPRD)   2 October 1949 until 13 November 1949

The return working was the 4.50 pm from Birmingham S.H. (Kidderminster 5.32 pm)

PASSENGER SERVICES

Birmingham and South Wales Expresses

8.30 am Cardiff to Birmingham S.H
Kidderminster 11.28 am

This train returned on the 5.0 pm from Birmingham S.H to Cardiff (Kidderminster 5.40 pm) and conveyed a Palethorpes' Sausage Van in each direction.

The locomotives on this service did not change very often. Regular ones were :

During 1940	5965 *Woollas Hall* (HFD) and 5988 *Bostock Hall* (HFD)
1941/42	6921 un-named (HFD) and 6935 un-named (HFD)
1945	4079 *Pendennis Castle* (HFD) and 6961 un-named (HFD)
1948/49	6984 *Owsden Hall* (HFD) and 6989 *Whitwick Hall* (HFD)

Authors collection

Palethorpes' Van as conveyed on South Wales train through Kidderminster

Trains between Birmingham S.H and South Wales and return were very busy at weekends, often running in several parts, and the main part with up to 16 coaches. The first part of the 8.0 am Birmingham to Cardiff often running non stop to Worcester.

27

Birmingham and South Wales Expresses

31 March 1945

    4096 *Highclere Castle* (BL)   1st part 1.40 pm (1.0 pm Birmingham S.H) to Cardiff

    2920 *Saint David* (HFD)   2nd part

19 May 1945

    6850 *Cleeve Grange* (BL)   1st part 8.35 am (8.0 am Birmingham S.H) to Cardiff

24 May 1947

    6866 *Morfa Grange* (TYS)   1st part 8.35 am (8.0 am Birmingham S.H) to Cardiff

    6860 *Aberporth Grange* (TYS)   2nd part

18 May 1948

    4941 *Llangedwyn Hall* (NPT)   1st part 4.30 pm (1.10 pm Cardiff) to Birmingham S.H

23 July 1948

    2951 *Tawstock Court* (HFD)   5.42 pm (5.0 pm Birmingham S.H) to Cardiff

24 July 1948

    5997 *Sparkford Hall* (TYS)   1st part 8.35 am (8.0 am Birmingham S.H) to Cardiff

    4924 *Eydon Hall* (TYS)   2nd part

    6871 *Bourton Grange* (PPRD)   1st part 11.26 am (8.30 am Cardiff) to Birmingham S.H

    6984 *Owsden Hall* (HFD)   2nd part

    7301 (WOS)   1st part 12.53 pm (9.48 am Cardiff) to Birmingham S.H

    4924 *Eydon Hall* (TYS)   2nd part

    6306 (WOS)   1st part 4.36 pm (1.10 pm Cardiff) to Birmingham S.H

    4917 *Crosswood Hall* (TYS)   2nd part

25 July 1948 (Sun)

    6837 *Forthampton Grange* (SPM)   1st part 12.35 pm (11.50 am Birmingham S.H) to Cardiff

    4992 *Crosby Hall* (TYS)   2nd part

    6856 *Stowe Grange* (SRD)   1st part 4.21 p.m to Birmingham S.H

    4992 *Crosby Hall* (TYS)   2nd part

31 July 1948

    4913 *Baglan Hall* (CDF)   1st part 8.35 am {8.0 a.m Birmingham S.H) to Cardiff

    4924 *Eydon Hall* (TYS)   2nd part

    4051 *Princess Helena* (HFD)   1st part 11.26 am (8.30 am Cardiff) to Birmingham S.H

    7308 (WOS)   2nd part

    6984 *Owsden Hall* (HFD)   3rd part

    6916 *Misterton Hall*   1st part 12.53 pm (9.48 am Cardiff) to Birmingham S.H

    4924 *Eydon Hall*   2nd part

    6950 *Kingsthorpe Hall (WOS)*   1st part 4.36 pm (1.10 pm Cardiff) to Birmingham S.H

    4913 *Baglan Hall* (CDF)   2nd part

    4992 *Crosby Hall* (TYS)   3rd part

7 August 1948

    4051 *Princess Helena* (HFD)   1st part 11.26 am (8.30 am Cardiff) to Birmingham S.H

    6877 *Llanfair Grange* (WOS)   2nd part

    6984 *Owsden Hall* (HFD)   3rd part

    4007 *Swallowfield Park* (WOS)   1st part 12.53 p.m (9.48 am Cardiff) to Birmingham S.H

    4917 *Crosswood Hall* (TYS)   2nd part

    6862 *Derwent Grange* (OXY)   1st part 4.36 pm (1.10 pm Cardiff) to Birmingham S.H

    4935 *Ketley Hall* (PDN)   2nd part

    4924 *Eydon Hall* (TYS)   3rd part

8 August 1948 (Sun)

    5004 *Llanstephan Castle* (PDN)   1st part 12.35 pm (11.50 am Birmingham S.H) to Cardiff

    4917 *Crosswood Hall* (TYS)   2nd part

14 August 1948

    2906 *Lady of Lynn* (CDF)   1st part 11.26 am (8.30 am Cardiff) to Birmingham S.H

    6989 *Wightwick Hall* (HFD)   2nd part

Cardiff to Birmingham expresses

Peter F. Curtis

4051 *Princess Helena* on 11.28 am to Birmingham S.H in 1947

Peter F. Curtis

6984 *Owsden Hall* on 11.28 am to Birmingham S.H
1 May 1948

PASSENGER SERVICES

Hereford to Birmingham S.H.

During the 1940s the Hereford to Birmingham trains were dominated by the 'Saint' class 4-6-0s. Hereford had at least half a dozen at any one time.

In 1942 Hereford had the following :

2920 *Saint David*	2924 *Saint Helena*	2932 *Ashton Court*
2938 *Corsham Court*	2944 *Highnam Court*	2951 *Tawstock Court*
2980 *Coeur de Lion*	2987 *Bride of Lammermoor*	

2937 *Clevedon Court* and 2948 *Stackpole Court* were also at Hereford from the mid 1940s replacing 2938, 2980 and 2987.

Tyseley had   2903 *Lady of Lyons* and 2916 *Saint Benedict*

Noted on the 8.10 pm Birmingham S.H to Hereford (Kidderminster 8.57 pm)

16 March 1945   2920 *Saint David* (HFD)
21 March 1945   2944 *Highnam Court* (HFD)
22 March 1945   2987 *Bride of Lammermoor* (HFD)
23 March 1945   2916 *Saint Benedict* (TYS)
24 March 1945   2948 *Stackpole Court* (HFD)
28 March 1945   6961 un-named (HFD)

Peter F Curtis

2951 *Tawstock Court* on 11.58 am to Hereford. April 1948

30

LOCAL PASSENGER SERVICES

Early morning commuter services usually consisted of a large prairie tank (51XX) and a Birmingham Division 4 coach non-corridor set. Five Birmingham Division sets were stabled overnight in the carriage sidings to the south of the station. These were cleaned internally and externally each evening.

Train		loco / shed	
5.45 am	Birmingham S.H.	2-6-2T	KDR
6.14 am	Birmingham S.H (6.0 am ex Bewdley)	2-6-2T	KDR
6.50 am	Wolverhampton	2-6-2T	SRD **
7.10 am	Birmingham S.H (6.33 am ex Worcester S.H)	4-6-0	WOS
7.32 am	Wolverhampton *	2-6-2T	SRD
7.43 am	Small Heath (7.30 am ex Bewdley)	2-6-2T	TYS
8.0 am	Birmingham S.H.	2-6-2T	KDR
8.19 am	Birmingham S.H. (7.10 am ex Ledbury)	2-6-2T	WOS
8.24 am	Birmingham S.H.	2-6-2T	TYS

*   this service commenced October 1946
** KDR loco from October 1946

Kidderminster used large prairie tanks 5110, 5112 and 8101, small prairies 4586, 4594, 4596, 5518 and 5573 on these services.

The 7.10 am to Birmingham S.H was usually hauled by a Worcester Hall or Grange. Regulars being 5914 *Ripon Hall*, 5917 *Westminster Hall*, 5983 *Henley Hall*, 6807 *Birchwood Grange*, 6851 *Hurst Grange* and 6877 *Llanfair Grange*. Exceptions noted included :

5 March 1947	2-6-0	9314 (OXY)
7 March 1947	4-6-0	6858 *Woolston Grange* (TYS)
12 May 1948	4-6-0	4052 *Princess Beatrice* (WOS)
22 October 1948	2-6-0	6395 (HFD)
21 December 1948	4-6-0	1010 *County of Carnarvan* (PDN)
21 September 1949	4-6-0	2947 *Madresfield Court* (CDF)

The 7.32 am to Wolverhampton usually had a Stafford Road large prairie but occasionally produced a locomotive ex works :

17 March 1947	0-6-0PT	8729 (BAN)
19 May 1947	0-6-0PT	3662 (NPT)

The Tyseley turns were worked by one of their many large prairie tanks.

The top Kidderminster Prairie Tank working was the 5.40 pm Birmingham Snow Hill to Malvern Wells calling at Smethwick Junction (to pick up only), Stourbridge Junction, Kidderminster, Droitwich Spa, Worcester ForegateStreet and the Malverns.This must have been one of the few workings where a Prairie Tank carried express passenger headlamps. 5110, 5112 and 8101 were the usual locomotives used.

8.15 am Shrewsbury to Birmingham
3.15 pm Stourbridge Jc. to Hartlebury
6.10 pm Hartlebury to Shrewsbury

In the early 1940s these services were worked mainly by Dean Goods 0-6-0 and Collett 0-6-0 locomotives from Shrewsbury and Stourbridge.

By 1944 these workings had been taken over by the Duke and Dukedog 4-4-0s.from Stourbridge and Shrewsbury . The regular locomotives were Dukes 3276 *Mounts Bay* and the un-named 3276 and Dukedog 3224 all SALOP, together with Duke 3284 *Isle of Jersey* and Dukedog 3208 from STB. After working the 8.15 a.m from Shrewsbury as far as Stourbridge the locomotive would spend the rest of the day as station pilot at Stourbridge Junction station. They were all renumbered into the 90XX series during the latter part of 1946.

During 1947 the locomotive which had worked on the 8.15 am passenger from Shrewsbury to Birmingham as far as Stourbridge Junction also worked local passenger trains between Birmingham and Kidderminster, finishing at Kidderminster at 11.04 pm and going on to KDR shed. It then worked the 8.00 am passenger to Birmingham before returning to Shrewsbury on the 6.10 pm Hartlebury to Shrewsbury. The locomotives used were the recently renumbered Duke and Dukedog 4-4-0s.

Friday 7 March 1947	9073 *Mounts Bay* (SALOP)	8.00 am to Birmingham S.H.
Saturday 8 March 1947	9073 *Mounts Bay* (SALOP)	10.28 am to Birmingham S.H.
	9084 *Isle of Jersey* (STB)	3.25 pm to Hartlebury
Monday 10 March 1947	9073 *Mounts Bay* (SALOP)	8.00 am to Birmingham S.H.
Saturday 22 March 1947	9076 (SALOP)	10.28 am to Birmingham S.H.
Easter Monday 7 April 1947	9019 (TYS)	10.28 am to Birmingham S.H.
Saturday 12 April 1947	9076 (SALOP)	10.28 am to Birmingham S.H.
Thursday 24 April 1947	9076 (SALOP)	8.00 am to Birmingham S.H.
Saturday 26 April 1947	9019 (TYS)	
Whit Monday 26 May 1947	9024 (SALOP)	10.28 am to Birmingham S.H.
Saturday 30 August 1947	9008 (TYS)	

By 1948 the 4-4-0 Dukes and Dukedogs had disappeared from these workings. The 8.15 am Shrewsbury to Birmingham and the 6.10 pm Hartlebury to Shrewsbury being worked by Stourbridge and Salop 2-6-2T on alternate days.

17 May 1948	4118 (SALOP)	10.28 am to Birmingham
	4146 (STB)	3.25 pm to Hartlebury
18 May 1948	4146 (STB)	10.28 am to Birmingham
24 July 1948	4118 (SALOP)	3.25 pm to Hartlebury
2 October 1948	5180 (STB)	10.28 am to Birmingham
9 October 1948	5191 (STB)	10.28 am to Birmingham
20 November 1948	4149 (STB)	10.28 am to Birmingham
	5168 (SALOP)	3.25 pm to Hartlebury
1 January 1949	5154 (SALOP)	10.28 am to Birmingham
18 April 1949	5168 (SALOP)	10.28 am to Birmingham
6 June 1949	4118 (SALOP)	10.28 am to Birmingham

Peter F. Curtis

Duke 3284 *Isle of Jersey* at Kidderminster on 3.25 p.m to Hartlebury in1946

Peter F. Curtis

Duke 9076 at Kidderminster on 10.28 a.m to Birmingham in 1947.

Peter F.Curtis

4110 on local train to Birmingham August 1947

Peter F.Curtis

2279 on 10.28 am local train to Birmingham
20 August 1946

"THE BEWDLEY BANJO"

'The Bewdley Banjo' was the local name for the auto train which operated on the Bewdley triangle and up as far as Bridgnorth. The usual locomotive used was 0-4-2T 4845, The spare locomotive being auto fitted 0-6-0T 6430. The auto coach was usually No.44.

In July 1941 this service was taken over by diesel railcars based at Worcester. However for the Bank holiday on 4 August the auto train was put back into service for one day with locomotive 4806 (WOS) and two auto coaches..

Although the auto train no longer operated, the auto coach remained at Kidderminster for several more years, being used to strengthen Birmingham services and used as a trailer for the Woofferton railcar as required. A 'Cordon' travelling gas tank wagon was stabled in the carriage siding to supply gas for the auto coach lighting.

The 1940 timetable was as follows :

> 5.40 am Kidderminster to Highley
> 6.15 am Highley to Kidderminster
> 6.50 am Kidderminster to Highley
> 7.17 am Highley to Bewdley
> 7.45 am Bewdley to Hartlebury
> 8.13 am Hartlebury to Bewdley
> 8.32 am Bewdley to Hartlebury
> 8.50 am Hartlebury to Bewdley to Kidderminster
>   ECS (SO) Kidderminster to Hartlebury
> 12.20 pm (SO) Hartlebury to Kidderminster
> 12.40 pm (SO) Kidderminster to Highley
> 1.45 pm (SO) Highley to Bewdley
> 1.30 pm (SX) Kidderminster to Bewdley
> 2.07 pm Bewdley to Hartlebury
> 2.35 pm Hartlebury to Highley
> 3.15 pm Highley to Kidderminster
> 3.45 pm Kidderminster to Bridgnorth
> 4.35 pm Bridgnorth to Kidderminster
>   ECS Kidderminster to Hartlebury
> 5.35 pm Hartlebury to Bewdley to Kidderminster
> 6.40 pm Kidderminster to Bewdley to Hartlebury
> 7.22 pm Hartlebury to Bewdley to Kidderminster
> 8.15 pm Kidderminster to Bridgnorth
> 9.20 pm Bridgnorth to Kidderminster

Another auto train working to Kidderminster was Worcester based.
> 7.14 am Kidderminster to Henwick
> 6.20 pm Colwall to Kidderminster
> 7.35 pm Kidderminster to Worcester F.S.

Locomotives noted on this service included :

12 February 1940	4818 (WOS)	20 March 1940	4804 (WOS)
20 September 1941	4860 (HFD)	6 May 1945	4818 (WOS)
8 October 1945	4822 (PPRD)	12 December 1946	1424 (GLO)
26 May 1947	1408 (WOS)	29 May 1947	1409 (LYD)

Kidderminster Railway Museum / V.R.Webster

4845 on auto train at Worcester Shrub Hill   14 August 1943

John Lewis collection

Auto coach No. 44 at Old Hill station.
The former Kidderminster Auto coach had been transferred to Stourbridge
by the time this photograph had been taken.

H.M.R.S Collection / P.J. Garland

Cordon Gas Tank Wagon

A similar wagon was stabled in the carriage sidings against the buffer stops to service the Auto Trailer.

The Kidderminster Gas Tank Wagon was sent to Worcester attached to a local passenger train to be refilled at the GWR Gas Works. These tanks were not permitted to be conveyed by goods trains or express passenger trains or be rough shunted to avoid leakages due to movement of the tanks on the bolsters.

BRANCH PASSENGER SERVICES

10.35 am Kidderminster to Shrewsbury

This service usually consisted of a Kidderminster 45XX 2-6-2T and three corridor coaches. On Saturdays and Bank Holiday Mondays a 2-6-0 was often used.

22 May 1945	5573 (KDR)	5 August 1946	4664 (KDR)
7 April 1947	9076 (SALOP)	26 May 1947	5303 (KDR)
17 May 1948	4586 (KDR)	2 August 1948	4584 (KDR)
2 October 1948	3607 (WOS)	9 October 1948	4584 (KDR)
20 November 1948	4614 (WOS)	27 December 1948	5105 (STB)
1 January 1949	4139 (WOS)	18 April 1949	4586 (KDR)
6 June 1949	6382 (KDR)		

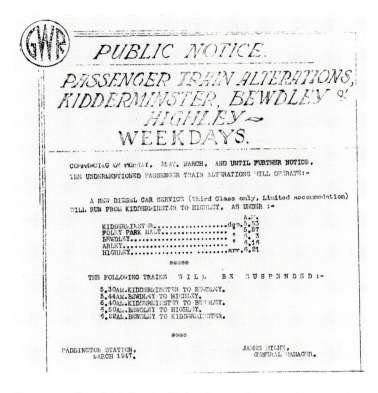

Commencing 31 March 1947 the early morning services for
the miners to Highley and Alveley were revised.
The Alveley stop was not advertised to the general public

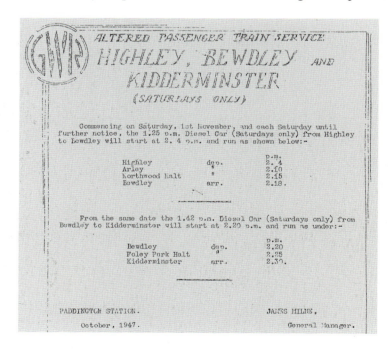

Commencing 1 November 1947 the afternoon train to
Highley and Alveley was retimed

BRANCH PASSENGER SERVICES

10.16 a.m and 1.50 p.m Kidderminster to Woofferton

Prior to the introduction of diesel railcars on these services on 18 August 1941 these trains were worked by locomotives from Ludlow shed. Ludlow was a sub shed of Shrewsbury which provided either 2-6-2T, 2-4-0T or 0-4-2Ts for the Kidderminster services. Locomotives noted were :

31 January 1940	2-4-0T	3563	1 February 1940	0-4-2T	3578
25 March 1940	2-6-2T	4511	1 May 1940	2-6-2T	4511
8 December 1940	2-4-0T	3561	16 December 1940	0-4-2T	3575
14 April 1941	0-4-2T	3579	16 August 1941	0-4-2T	3575

The stock consisted of two clerestory non corridor coaches with boards branded Woofferton.

Commencing on Monday 18 August 1941 these services were taken over by Railcars Nos 25 and 33 from Worcester. Railcar No. 33 had been previously noted on the line on 14 July 1941 hauling two coaches on a test run.

On summer Saturdays and Bank Holidays the services reverted to steam usually with a Kidderminster 45XX 2-6-2T.

22 May 1945	4534 (HFD on loan KDR)	5 August 1946	4629 (KDR)
26 May 1947	5518 (KDR)	2 August 1948	5544 (KDR)
18 April 1949	4584 (KDR)	6 June 1949	4153 (KDR)
10 September 1949	4586 (KDR)		

Peter F. Curtis

5518 in Yew Tree Road Siding   1946

GREAT WESTERN RAILWAY
AND
MIDLAND "RED"
Combined Rail and Road Services

ALTERNATIVE AVAILABILITY OF RAIL TICKETS

Commencing on OCTOBER 6th, 1947, and until further notice, passengers holding ordinary single or monthly return rail tickets from or to points **beyond**

KIDDERMINSTER

to or from the undermentioned points, may travel by Midland " Red " Bus Services between these points and Kidderminster when there is no connecting train service available :

STOURPORT-ON-SEVERN
BEWDLEY
WYRE FOREST (For FAR FOREST)
CLEOBURY MORTIMER
NEWNHAM BRIDGE
TENBURY WELLS.

Subject to the Rules and Regulations shewn in the Omnibus Company's Official Time Tables.

Passengers accompanied luggage will be conveyed in the buses where sufficient accommodation is available in accordance with the regulation of the Omnibus Company as shewn in their official time table.

D. M. SINCLAIR, General Manager,	JAMES MILNE, General Manager,
B. & M.M.O, Co., Ltd.,	G.W.R.,
Bearwood,	Paddington Station.
Birmingham.	*September*, 1947.

From September 1947 passengers holding tickets issued to or from points beyond Kidderminster were able to travel by 'Midland Red' bus when there was no connecting train service available. This facility was short lived, however, lasting until 1949.

R.S.Carpenter / J. Scott-Morgan collection
A.E.C Railcar No. 7 at Malvern Wells c1946

The Diesel Railcars

R.S.Carpenter

Railcar No.20

The diesel railcars came into regular service in the Kidderminster area in July 1941, taking over from the local auto train and certain Woofferton services. The railcars were Worcester based, there being no servicing facilities at Kidderminster.

There were two types of diesel railcar :
    1. The 'Streamline' ones built by AEC at Southall numbered 1 to 18.
    2. The Swindon built ones numbered 19 to 38

Prior to July 1941 Nos. 5, 6 and 7 were to be seen on local services from Worcester.

Railcar No. 33 was the first of the Swindon ones to be noted on 14 July 1941, hauling two coaches, presumably on a test run. Two weeks later on 30 July Nos. 22 and 23 were noted on test runs.

The railcars were frequently swapped and others seen on local services were :

No. 14 21 April 1942	No. 26 11 April 1942	No. 27 17 December 1943
No. 28 7 August 1945	No. 29 12 June 1942	No. 30 8 October 1943
No. 32 6 March 1947		

For a short time in 1944 Nos 6 and 33 were loaned to the LNER to work in the Newcastle area.

At 8.21 am on 2 July 1949 Railcar No. 33 was noted on a Stephenson Locomotive Society special from Birmingham to Welshpool via the Severn Valley.

SEASIDE EXCURSION

SUNDAY, JULY 3rd

SPECIAL HALF-DAY EXCURSION

— TO —

NEWPORT   CARDIFF

(arrive 12.32 p.m.)   (GENERAL, arrive 12.53 p.m.)

AND

PORTHCAWL

(arrive 1.54 p.m.)

FROM	Depart	RETURN FARES, Third Class			Arrival on Return
		NEWPORT	CARDIFF	PORTHCAWL	
	a.m.	s. d.	s. d.	s. d.	p.m.
Kidderminster	9 45	9 0	10 0	13 6	12 0
Hartlebury	9 50	9 0	10 0	13 6	11 53
Droitwich Spa	10 5	8 6	9 6	13 0	11 42
Worcester (Foregate Street) ..	10 15	8 0	9 0	12 6	11 28
Henwick	10 20	8 0	9 0	12 6	11 25
Malvern Link	10 30	7 0	8 0	11 6	11 14
Great Malvern	10 35	7 0	8 0	11 6	11 9
Colwall	10 45	7 0	8 0	11 6	11 3
Ledbury	10 55	6 6	7 6	10 6	10 52

RETURN ARRANGEMENTS—SAME DAY
Porthcawl depart 7.55 p.m., Cardiff (General) depart 8.50 p.m. and Newport depart 9.10 p.m.

Children under Three years of age, Free ; Three and under Fourteen years, Half-fare.

FOR PARTICULARS OF EXCURSION TO RHYL—P.T.O.

Pamphlet advertising Half-Day excursion to Porthcawl on 3 July 1949.

EXCURSIONS

Day excursion trains suspended during the war years recommenced in 1948, some of those noted at Kidderminster in 1949 are listed below :

22 May 1949	5997 *Sparkford Hall* (TYS)	Weston Super Mare
29 May 1949	5970 *Hengrave Hall* (CDF)	Cardiff to Birmingham
5 June 1949	4007 *Swallowfield Park* (WOS)	9.55 am Kidderminster to Weston Super Mare
	5911 *Preston Hall* (NPT)	Birmingham to Barry Island
	4917 *Crosswood Hall* (TYS)	Birmingham to Barry Island
11 June 1949	4007 *Swallowfield Park* (WOS)	Kidderminster to Blackpool (Parsons Chain Ltd)
12 June 1949	4051 *Princess Helena* (WOS)	9.45 am Kidderminster to Barry Island
	5089 *Westminster Abbey* (LDR)	Swansea to Birmingham
18 June 1949	4900 *Saint Martin* (PDN)	Kidderminster to Paddington (British Legion)
19 June 1949	6843 *Poulton Grange* (TYS)	Birmingham to Weston Super Mare
	6858 *Woolston Grange* (TYS)	Birmingham to Barry Island
29 June 1949	6852 *Headbourne Grange* (SPM)	Wolverhampton to Weston Super Mare
3 July 1949	5917 *Westminster Hall* (WOS)	9.45 am Kidderminster to Porthcawl
10 July 1949	4047 *Princess Louise* (BL)	Birmingham to Weston Super Mare
17 July 1949	6938 *Corndean Hall* (WOS)	9.30 am Kidderminster to Weston Super Mare
	5993 *Kirby Hall* (TYS)	Birmingham to Barry Island
24 July 1949	7315 (SRD)	Wolverhampton to Weston Super Mare
	5970 *Hengrave Hall*	Birmingham to Weston Super Mare
	4039 *Queen Matilda* (LDR)	Swansea to Birmingham
7 August 1949	5932 *Haydon Hall* (PDN)	Wolverhampton to Weston Super Mare
	5907 *Marble Hall* (TYS)	Birmingham to Weston Super Mare
14 August 1949	6851 *Hurst Grange* (WOS)	9.45 am Kidderminster to Weston Super Mare
	5936 *Oakley Hall* (PDN)	Wolverhampton to Barry Island
	6843 *Poulton Grange* (TYS)	Birmingham to Barry Island
21 August 1949	5997 *Sparkford Hall* (TYS)	Birmingham to Weston Super Mare
	6963 *Throwley Hall* (SALOP)	Wolverhampton to Weston Super Mare
28 August 1949	6385 (WOS)	9.45 am Kidderminster to Barry Island
	4959 *Purley Hall* (TYS)	Birmingham to Porthcawl
17 Sept 1949	4051 *Princess Helena* (WOS)	Kidderminster to Paddington (SDF Ltd)
18 Sept 1949	4959 *Purley Hall* (TYS)	Birmingham to Weston Super Mare
	6877 *Llanfair Grange* (WOS)	9.45 am Kidderminster to Barry Island
25 Sept 1949	5993 *Kirby Hall* (TYS)	Birmingham to Porthcawl
1 Oct 1949	4051 *Princess Helena* (WOS)	7.20 am Kidderminster to Blackpool
	4007 *Swallowfield Park* (WOS)	8.00 am Kidderminster to Blackpool
2 Oct 1949	6904 *Charfield Hall* (TYS)	Birmingham to Cardiff
	6947 *Helmingham Hall* (WOS)	Fencote to Blackpool Central
16 Oct 1949	5993 *Kirby Hall* (TYS)	Birmingham to Cardiff
	5970 *Hengrave Hall*	Cardiff to Birmingham
23 Oct 1949	5927 *Guild Hall* (TYS)	Birmingham to Cardiff
	4923 *Evenley Hall* (PDN)	Paddington to Stourbridge Junc.
	4092 *Dunraven Castle* (WOS)	9.20 am Kidderminster to Paddington
20 Nov 1949	4048 *Princess Victoria* (LDR)	Swansea to Birmingham

The Kidderminster Co-op commenced running an annual excursion in 1948. The first was to Porthcawl on Wednesday 18 August. Fares were Adults 25/-, Children 12/6 including tea.

In 1949 the destination was Rhyl on Wednesday 27 July. Two trains were run carrying 700 passengers.

Cradley Speedway Excursions

In 1949 special evening excursions were run from Malvern Wells to Cradley Heath calling at principal stations to Kidderminster (6.50 pm) for the Speedway at the Dudley Wood Stadium. Returning from Cradley Heath at 9.45 pm.

13 May 1949	6306 (WOS)	27 May 1949	6851 *Hurst Grange* (WOS)		
10 June 1949	6306 (WOS)	17 June 1949	8106 (WOS)	24 June 1949	6378 (WOS)
1 July 1949	5396 (SDN)	8 July 1949	6378 (WOS)		
15 July 1949	4092 *Dunraven Castle* (WOS)			22 July 1949	4114 (WOS)
29 July 1949	8106 (WOS)	5 August 1949	6396 (WOS)	12 August 1949	6385 (WOS)
19 August 1949	8106 (WOS)	2 Sept 1949	6385 (WOS)	30 Sept 1949	8106 (WOS)
7 October 1949	4114 (WOS)				

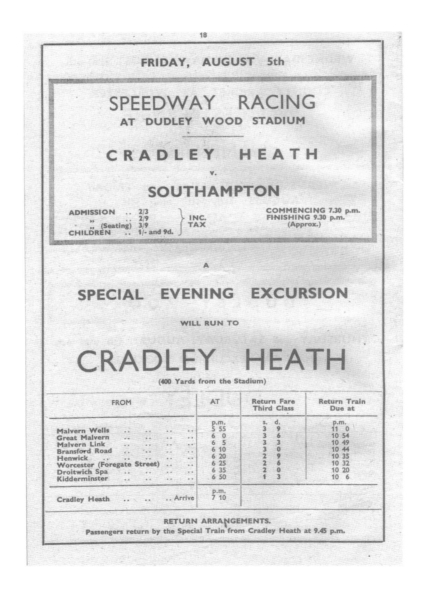

Local Football Excursions
Kidderminster Harriers

10 November 1948	Hereford to Birmingham S.H (11.40 am Kidder)	6989 *Whitwick Hall* (HFD)
27 November 1948	Hereford to Kidderminster (10 coaches) FA Cup	6905 *Charfield Hall* (HFD)
	Hereford to Kidderminster (10 coaches)	2944 *Highnam Court* (HFD)
27 December 1948	11.35 am Kidderminster to Hereford (via Woofferton)	4100 (KDR)
26 March 1949	Henwick to Kidderminster (10 coaches)	8106 (WOS)
9 April 1949	2.5 pm Kidderminster to Worcester Foregate Street	5110 (KDR)
19 April 1949	4.25 pm Kidderminster to Worcester Foregate Street	6385 (WOS)
14 May 1949	1.55 pm Henwick to Kidderminster (2.30 pm)	5173 (WOS) 12 coaches
17 September 1949	2.5 pm Kidderminster to Stourbridge	4149 (STB)
24 September 1949	Stourbridge to Kidderminster	4150 (STB)
26 November 1949	Henwick to Kidderminster (1.35 pm)	6938 *Corndean Hall* (WOS)
26 December 1949	Gloucester to Kidderminster (1.20 pm)	4996 *Eden Hall* (GLO)

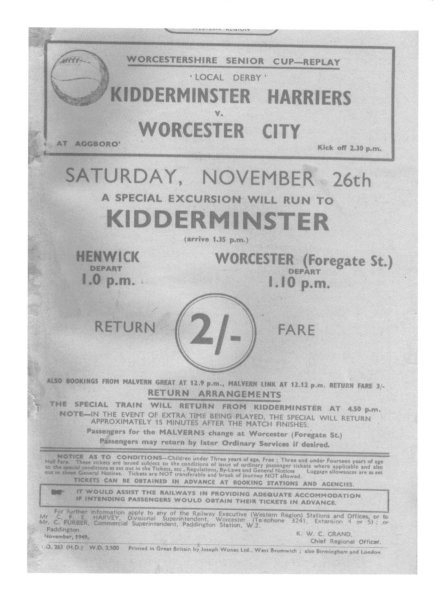

Other Football Excursions

24 April 1948	7.5 am Kidderminster to Paddington (FA Cup)	5088 *Llanthony Abbey* (SRD)
29 January 1949	Cardiff to Birmingham	6948 *Holbrooke Hall* (CDF)
30 April 1949	7.5 am Kidderminster to Paddington (FA Cup)	5015 *Kingswear Castle* (SRD)
17 September 1949	Newport to Walsall	5941 *Campion Hall* (NPT)
1 October 1949	12.45 pm Kidderminster to The Hawthorns	5303 (KDR)
15 October 1949	1.5 pm Kidderminster to Witton	4146 (STB)
29 October 1949	1.5 pm Kidderminster to Witton	5167 (STB)
12 November 1949	12.55 pm Kidderminster to Witton	5300 (STB) + 5147 (STB)
26 November 1949	1.0 pm Kidderminster to Witton	5165 (STB) + 5197 (STB)

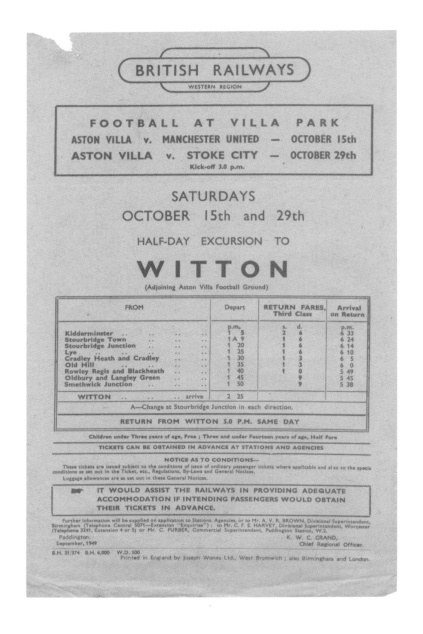

Worcester Races

29 May 1948	Birmingham S.H to Worcester F.S	(12.50 pm Kidder)	6866 *Morfa Grange* (TYS)
10 July 1948	Birmingham S.H to Worcester F.S	(12.50 pm Kidder)	6336 (TYS)
25 September 1948	Birmingham S.H to Worcester F.S	(12.50 pm Kidder)	6833 *Calcot Grange* (TYS)
30 October 1948	Birmingham S.H to Worcester F.S	(12.25 pm Kidder)	6866 *Morfa Grange* (TYS)
13 August 1949	Birmingham S.H to Worcester F.S	(12.50 pm Kidder)	5944 *Ickenham Hall* (SRD)

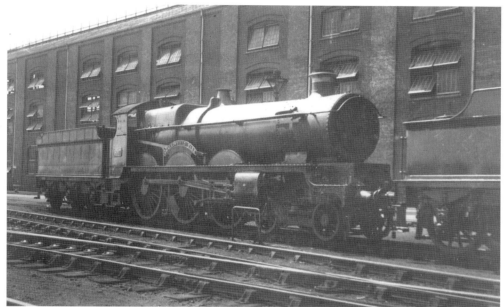

Photo : Stephenson Locomotive Society

Star Class 4-6-0 4007 *Swallowfield Park* at Swindon
This was a favourite on excursions from the Worcester area.

Summer Holiday Trains

Commencing with the 1949 summer timetable two Saturday only services were introduced.
Worcester S.H to Chester and Kidderminster to Barry Island.

2 July 1949	9.40 am to Chester	6936 *Breccles Hall* (WOS)
9 July 1949	7.50 am to Barry Island	6936 *Breccles Hall* (WOS)
	9.40 am to Chester	5017 *St. Donats Castle* (WOS)
16 July 1949	9.40 am to Chester	4051 *Princess Helena* (WOS)
23 July 1949	7.50 am to Barry Island	5914 *Ripon Hall* (WOS)
13 August 1949	7.50 am to Barry Island	6936 *Breccles Hall* (WOS)
	9.40 am to Chester	4007 *Swallowfield Park* (WOS)
20 August 1949	7.50 am to Barry Island	6807 *Birchwood Grange* (WOS)
	9.40 am to Chester	5063 *Earl Baldwin* (WOS)
27 August 1949	7.50 am to Barry Island	7806 *Cockington Manor* (BAN)
	9.40 am to Chester	4052 *Princess Beatrice* (WOS)

Bank Holiday Mondays

Stourport-on-Severn was always an attraction for Birmingham and Black Country people and thousands travelled by train there every Bank Holiday. The war years were no exception. Extra trains being run to cater for the crowds. In August 1940 the *Kidderminster Shuttle* reported that the railway conveyed 7,000 passengers to Bewdley and Stourport on Severn on the Bank Holiday Monday. At 11.15 pm there were still 200 waiting for a train at Stourport to take them home.

A typical morning / afternoon observation on August Bank Holiday Monday 5 August 1946 taken at Kidderminster :

8.0 am	4641 (WOS)	off shed
8.2 am	7315 (SRD)	Wolverhampton to Paddington
8.19 am	4139 (WOS)	Ledbury to Birmingham Snow Hill.
8.35 am	4917 *Crosswood Hall* (TYS)	Birmingham Snow Hill to Cardiff
	2274 (WOS)	Goods from Worcester
8.53 am	2944 *Highnam Court* (HFD)	Hereford to Birmingham Snow Hill
8.45 am	4641 (WOS)	Kidderminste to Woofferton
	4629 (KDR)	off shed
9.10 am	Railcar 28 (WOS)	Woofferton to Kidderminster
9.25 am	4051 *Princess Helena* (WOS)	Hereford to Birmingham Snow Hill
9.33 am	5075 *Wellington* (SRD)	Wolverhampton to Oxford
9.50 am	5134 (STB)	Special to Bewdley and Stourport
	4664 (KDR)	off shed
9.58 am	4139 (WOS)	Birmingham Snow Hill to Kidderminster
10.8 am	7315 (SRD)	Worcester Shrub Hill to Crewe
	4629 (KDR)	Kidderminster to Woofferton
10.16 am	2234 (SALOP)	Shrewsbury to Birmingham Snow Hill
	5134 (STB)	ECS from Stourport via Hartlebury
10.28 am	2916 *Saint Benedict* (TYS)	Birmingham Snow Hill to Hereford
10.38 am	4664 (KDR)	Kidderminster to Shrewsbury
10.40 am	5198 (TYS)	Birmingham Snow Hil to Stourport
11.0 am	6860 *Aberporth Grange* (TYS)	Wolverhampton to Evesham
11.12 am	4641 (WOS)	Woofferton to Kidderminster
11.15 am	9733 (TYS)	Birmingham Snow Hill to Stourport
11.16 am	2924 *Saint Helena* (WOS)	Cardiff to Birmingham Snow Hill
11.28 am	6921 (WOS) un-named	Wolverhampton to Worcester Shrub Hill
	5125 (TYS)	Birmingham Snow Hill to Malvern
	5198 (TYS)	ECS from Stourport via Hartlebury
	7811 *Dunley Manor* (BAN)	Wolverhampton to Malvern
12.44	8727 (KDR	Birmingham Snow Hill to Stourport
12.53 pm	4917 *Crosswood Hall* (TYS)	Hereford to Birmingham Snow Hill
	4139 (WOS)	off shed to Hartlebury
	9608 (TYS)	Birmingham Snow Hill to Stourport
1.11 pm	4629 (KDR)	Woofferton to Kidderminster
	5196 (STB)	Wolverhampton to Stourport
1.2 pm	5045 *Earl of Dudley* (SRD)	Wolverhampton to Paddington
1.30 pm	6396 (WOS)	Kidderminster to Birmingham Snow Hill
1.40 pm	4051 *Princess Helena* (WOS)	Birmingham Snow Hill to Cardiff
	5112 (KDR)	Birmingham to Stourport
2.10 pm	4641 (WOS)	Kidderminster to Woofferton
2.24 pm	4104 (STB)	Birmingham Snow Hill to Kidderminster
3.5 pm	4114 (WOS)	Wolverhampton to Paddington

BANK HOLIDAY MONDAYS

A typical evenings observation on Whitsuntide Bank Holiday Monday 17 May 1948 taken at Kidderminster.

5.5 pm	4153 (KDR)	Bridgnorth to Birmingham Snow Hill
5.42 pm	5983 *Henley Hall* (WOS)	Birmingham Snow Hill to Cardiff
5.55 pm	6920 *Barningham Hall* (HFD)	Hereford to Birmingham Snow Hill
5.58 pm	5110 (KDR)	Wolverhampton to Worcester Shrub Hill
	5197 (STB)	E.C.S Hartlebury & Stourport
	4150 (STB)	Stourport to Birmingham Snow Hill
6.19 pm	4100 (KDR)	Birmingham Snow Hill to Malvern Wells
6.25 pm	Railcar 32 (WOS)	Kidderminster to Woofferton
	6950 *Kingsthorpe Hall* (WOS)	Stourport to Birmingham Snow Hill
7.0 pm	5136 (STB)	E.C.S Hartlebury & Stourport
7.8 pm	4139 (WOS)	Worcester Shrub Hill to Wolverhampton
7.10 pm	5152 (TYS)	Stourport to Birmingham Snow Hill
7.14 pm	4153 (KDR)	Birmingham Snow Hill to Kidderminster
7.16 pm	5114 (WOS)	Shrewsbury to Birmingham Snow Hill
7.40 pm	4944 *Middleton Hall* (SRD)	Evesham to Wolverhampton
	5187 (TYS)	Stourport to Birmingham Snow Hill
	5197 (STB)	Stourport to Wolverhampton
8.10 pm	5173 (WOS)	Birmingham Snow Hill to Worcester S.H.
8.13 pm	5110 (KDR)	Paddington to Wolverhampton
	5909 *Newton Hall* (SRD)	Hereford to Wolverhampton
	5136 (STB)	Stouport to Birmingham Snow Hill
	4100 (KDR)	Malvern Wells to Birmingham Snow Hill
8.36 pm	2944 *Highnam Court* (HFD)	Hereford to Birmingham Snow Hill
	5138 (STB)	Stourport to Wolverhampton
8.55 pm	5544 (KDR)	Woofferton to Birmingham Snow Hill
8.57 pm	6920 *Barningham Hall* (HFD)	Birmingham Snow Hill to Hereford
	7318 (RDG)	Light engine

Excursions to Bewdley and Stourport from the Midland Region.

Commencing in September 1948 excursions were run from Walsall, Rugeley and Lichfield area to Bewdley and Stourport. The ex LMS locomotives were changed at Dudley for GWR 2-6-2Ts from Stourbridge. It was not until 1950 that the LMS locomotive ran right through.

Noted at Kidderminster were :

18 September 1948	5191 (STB)	reporting No. W731	to Bewdley	8 coaches
6 June 1949	5196 (STB)	reporting No. W978	Rugeley Town to Bewdley	11.25 am
2 July 1949	5170 (STB)	reporting No. W710	to Stourport	11.25 am
	4116 (TYS)		Rugeley to Stourport	1.15 pm
17 September 1949	4149 (STB)		to Bewdley	8.50 am

Bank Holidays at Stourport-on-Severn

A.J Turley

Bank Holiday crowds on the riverside at Stourport-on-Severn in the late 1940s

A.J Turley

Bank Holiday crowds arriving at Stourport-on-Severn station

Peter F.Curtis

4147 (TYS) on a Birmingham to Stourport special
17 May 1948

Peter F.Curtis

5197 (STB) on a Wolverhampton to Stourport special
17 May 1948

Sunday 29 May 1949

The following is a typical Sunday morning / afternoon observation. On this day there was single line working. 2270 (STB) and 6677 (STB) were pilot locos.

5156 (TYS)	8.34 am	Bridgnorth
5189 (STB)	9.8 am	Bewdley and Stourport
Railcar 32 (WOS)		P-way workmen to Kidderminster
1016 *County of Hants* (SRD)	9.37 am	Oxford
6342 (OXY)	10.5 am	goods (down)
2655 (STB)	10.8 am	goods (up)
6932 *Burwarton Hall* (PDN)	11.10 am	Birmingham Snow Hill
5110 (KDR)	11.8 am	Great Malvern
6385 (WOS)	11.24 am	Wolverhampton
3862 (PPRD)	11.55 am	goods (down)
5361 (BAN)	12.5 pm	goods (up)
5970 *Hengrave Hall* (CDF)		Cardiff to Birmingham S.H excursion
5997 *Sparkford Hall* (TYS)	12.35 pm	Cardiff
4963 *Rignall Hall*	1.15 pm	pigeon special to Malvern
6807 *Birchwood Grange* (WOS)	2.22 pm	Wolverhampton
4165 (TYS)	2.45 pm	Bewdley
4166 (TYS)	3.54 pm	Hartlebury
6984 *Owsden Hall* (HFD)	4.36 pm	Birmingham Snow Hill

8727 (KDR)   Kidderminster yard shunter   7700 (KDR)   Stourport shunter

A.J Turley

Dean Goods 0-6-0 2538 on a northbound goods 1947

Hop Pickers Specials

Special trains were run conveying families from the Black Country to the hop fields in the Tenbury Wells and Hereford areas. The stock usually consisted of old coaches and luggage vehicles.

The trains to Tenbury Wells were usually hauled by Collett 0-6-0s from Tyseley, 2203 and 2238 being noted.

Sample observations :

31 August 1947	6854 *Roundhill Grange* (BAN)	6855 *Saighton Grange* (TYS)
	5171 (TYS)	
1 September 1947	6855 *Saighton Grange* (TYS)	
2 September 1947	6952 *Kimberley Hall* (DID)	
4 September 1947	5375 (RDG)	
5 September 1948	6866 *Morfa Grange* (TYS)	5386 (SRD)
	6853 *Morehampton Grange* (TYS)	4967 *Shirenewton Hall* (TYS)
	5333 (OXY)	
28 August 1949	6955 *Lydcott Hall* (WES)	
29 August 1949	4337 (SRD) 11 coaches	5936 *Oakley Hall* (PDN) 14 coaches + 1 van
30 August 1949	2903 *Lady of Lyons* (TYS)	

Return Trains from Tenbury Wells :

24 September 1949	5160 (STB)
25 September 1949	3219 (WOS)

Other observations, dates unrecorded :

4964 *Rodwell Hall* (TYS)	5916 *Trinity Hall* (TYS)	6960 *Raveningham Hall* (PDN)
6981 *Marbury Hall* (BL)	7800 *Torquay Manor* (TYS)	

Pigeon Specials

A regular pigeon train during 1949 was from Wolverhampton to Malvern on Sundays passing through Kidderminster at 1.15 p.m.

1 May 1949	7315 (SRD)	10 July 1949	6848 *Toddington Grange* (SRD)
8 May 1949	4951 *Pendeford Hall* (PDN)	17 July 1949	6826 *Nannerth Grange* (SHL)
15 May 1949	5022 *Wigmore Castle* (SRD)	24 July 1949	6848 *Toddington Grange* (SRD)
29 May 1949	4963 *Rignall Hall* (WES)	7 August 1949	6846 *Ruckley Grange* (SPM)
5 June 1949	5945 *Leckhampton Hall* (SRD)	14 August 1949	7315 (SRD)
12 June 1949	7315 (SRD)	21 August 1949	6815 *Frilford Grange* (TN)
19 June 1949	7315 (SRD)	28 August 1949	6391 (SRD)
26 June 1949	7315 (SRD)		

GOODS TRAINS

Goods Train Classifications.

	Class C	Parcels, Fish, Meat, Fruit, Milk, Horse, Cattle, or Perishable Train, Composed entirely of Vacuum fitted stock, with the vacuum pipe connected to engine. Express Freight, Livestock, Perishable, or Ballast Train partly vacuum Fitted, with not less than one third vacuum braked vehicles connected by vacuum pipe to engine.
	Class D	Express Freight or Ballast Train conveying not less than 4 vacuum braked Vehicles connected by vacuum pipe to engine and authorised to run at a maximum speed of 35 mph.
	Class E	Express Freight, Fish, Meat, Fruit, Cattle or BallastTrain not running under "C" or "D" Head Lamp conditions.
	Class F	Through Fast Freight Train not running under "C", "D" or "E" Head Lamp conditions, conveying through load.
	Class G	Light Engine or Light Engines coupled together, or Engine and Brake.
	Class H	Freight, Mineral or Ballast Train or Train of Empties carrying through load to destination.
	Class J	Through Freight, Mineral or Ballast Train stopping at intermediate stations.
	Class K	Ordinary Freight, Mineral or Ballast Train stopping at local stations. Branch Freight.

Goods Trains at Kidderminster in 1942

Weekdays

Time KDR		Class	
12.7/1.31 am		F	10.0 pm Hollinswood - Worcester
12.25 am	MX	K	Stourbridge Junc. – Worcester
12.39 am	MWFO	H	11.10 pm Cannock Road – Pontypool Road (loco coal empties)
1.23 am	MX	F	10.0 pm Bordesley Junc.– Worcester
1.35 am			8.35 pm Panteg – Stourbridge Junct. (Thurs & Sat)
			Wolverhampton (Tues & Fri)
1.44/2.0 am	MX	K	1.30 am Hartlebury _ Kingswinford
1.51 am		F	9.50 am Victoria Basin – Cardiff
2.28 am	MX	F	11.25 pm Hereford – Bordesley Junc.
2.53 am	MO	F	2.35 am Stourbridge Junc. – Pontypool Road
2.57/3.7 am	MX	F	11.30 pm Bordesley Junc. – Pontypool Road
3.4 am	MO	E	10.15 pm Cardiff – Bordesley Junc.
3.17 am	MX RR	E	11.42 pm Morris Cowley – Crewe
3.30 am		F	3.30 am Kidderminster – Cardiff empties
3.34 am	MO	H	1.15 am Cannock Road – Pontypool Road
3.35/3.55 am		E	9.35 pm Crewe – Worcester
3.57/4.38 am		F	3.15 am Worcester – Market Drayton
4.5 am	MX	E	12.50 am Crewe – Bristol
4.40/4.55 am	MO	F	4.0 am Worcester – Oxley Sidings
4.32/4.55 am	MX	J	4.10 am Stourbridge Junc. – Hartlebury
4.54/5.30 am	T,Th,SO	J	3.15 am Great Bridge – Worcester
6.25 am		F	9.55 pm Cardiff – Oxley Sidings
7.50 am		E	5.10am Oxley Sidings – Worcester
8.35 am	MX	F	8.45 pm Margam – Oxley Sidings
9.5 am		F	7.25 am Worcester –Kidderminster
9.40/11.0 am		F	8.36 am Stourbridge Junc. – Tenbury & Hereford
9.45 am		H	9.25 am Stourbridge Junc. – Cwmbach
10.25 am		E	6.33 am Crewe – Moreton Cutting
10.43 am		H	4.35 am Pontypool Road – Oxley Sidings
10.50 am		H	10.30 am Stourbridge Junc. – Pontypool Road
11.0 am	RR SX *	K	11.0 am Kidderminster – Newnham Bridge
11.38 /12.10 pm		K	9.0 amTipton –Hartlebury (No.7 Bank)
11.52/12.2 pm		H	5.25 am Pontypool Road – Oxley Sidings
12.0 noon		K	Bewdley – Kidderminster
12.0 noon	SX	K	12.0 Kidderminster – Highley
12.2 pm		F	10.15 am Hollinswood – Swindon
12.20 pm		K	11.40 am Kingswinford – Elmley Lovett
1.55 pm		H	10.55 am Cannock Road – Pontypool Road
2.2 pm		K	1.45 pm Elmley Lovett – Stourbridge Junc.
2.58 pm		E	11.15 am Didcot – Oxley Sidings
3.6/3.40 pm		F	9.25 am Basingstoke – Oxley Sidings
3.23 pm	RR	C	12.20 pm Long Marston – Oxley Sidings
3.33/3.52 pm		H	9.0 am Pontypool Road – Stourbridge Junction
5.7 pm		E	1.35 pm Crewe – Stoke Gifford
5.18 pm		H	10.30 am Penarth Curve – Stourbridge Junc.
5.55 pm		C	2.10 pm Littleton & Badsey – Crewe
7.0 pm		K	8.20 am Shrewsbury Coton Hill – Kidderminster
7.39 pm	TFO	H	12.30 pm Panteg – Stourbridge Junc.
7.49/8.4 pm		H	6.15 pm Great Bridge – Hartlebury
8.10 pm		F	5.0 pm Worcester – Kidderminster
8.12 pm	SO	F	8.12 pm Kidderminster – Worcester

Time KDR		Class	
8.20 pm	SX	C	8.20 pm Kidderminster – Paddington
8.35 pm	RR	C	8.35pm Kidderminster – Crewe
8.41/9.5 pm		H	1.10 pm Alexandra Dock Junc. – Stourbridge Junc.
9.3/9.28 pm	SX	C	8.35 pm Worcester – Crewe
9.11/9.25 pm	SO	F	8.35 pm Worcester – Crewe
10.0/11.15 pm		K	6.0 pm Tenbury – Stourbridge Junc.
10.10 pm	SX	F	10.10 pm Kidderminster – Worcester
10.20/10.54 pm		E	9.45 pm Worcester - Crewe
10.55 pm		F	7.40 pm Cannock Road – Reading
11.15/11.37 pm	RR	E	10.30 pm Worcester – Crewe
11.50 pm		H	11.30 pm Stourbridge Junc – Pontypool Road

Sundays

Time	Class	
12.15 am	H	6.20 pm Pontypool Road – Oxley Sidings
1.23am	F	10.0 pm Bordesley Junc – Pontypool Road
1.35 am	H	8.35 pm Panteg – Stourbridge Junc.
1.36 am	E	9.50 pm Victoria Basin – Cardiff
1.44/2.0 am	K	1.30 am Hartlebury – Stourbridge Junc
2.12 am	F	10.25 pm Oxley Sidings – Pontypool Road
2.35 am	F	11.30 pm Bordesley Junction – Pontypool Road
2.50 am	J	6.45 pm Oxford – Stourbridge Junc.
3.30 am	E	3.30 am Kidderminster – Cardiff
3.35/3.55 am	E	9.55 pm Crewe – Worcester
4.5 am	E	12.50 am Crewe – Bristol
6.25 am	F	9.55 pm Cardiff – Oxley Sidings
6.28 /6.43 am	F	4.20 am Oxley Sidings – Worcester
8.15 am	F	9.10 pm Llandilo – Stourbridge Junc
9.54 am	E	8.30 am Hockley – Cardiff
10.11/10.25	F	11.45 pm Margam – Oxley Sidings

RR = Run when required only
SO = Saturdays only
MX = Mondays excepted
T = Tuesdays   W = Wednesdays

SX = Saturdays excepted
MO = Mondays only
Th = Thursdays   F = Fridays

* combined with Tenbury/Hereford goods as far as Bewdley then independently from Bewdley to Newnham Bridge handling traffic for Ditton Priors Naval Depot.

In addition to the regular goods trains listed above there were numerous Government Stores trains conveying military equipment. There were also trains conveying seasonal traffic such as sugar beet, potatoes and broccoli.

Working Timetables were issued twice yearly, usually in May and October. The times of regular goods trains were frequently changed. Some services discontinued and others added.

The following pages give details of the locomotives that were observed on some of the regular services. In wartime in particular it was difficult to identify which train it was as very often they were hours late, priority being given to Government Stores trains.

"The Carpet"
8.20 pm Kidderminster to Paddington   Class C

In the early 1930s the GWR named most of their overnight express fitted freights. One of these was the 8.20 pm Kidderminster to Paddington, which was known as "The Carpet". In 1940 the locomotive for this train was usually a Paddington Castle, which had worked to Kidderminster on a local passenger train from Birmingham.

Date	No.	Name	Shed	Date	No.	Name	Shed
10 April 1940	4907	*Broughton Hall*	(PDN)	1 Aug 1940	4912	*Berrington Hall*	(PPRD)
11 April 1940	5019	*Treago Castle*	(PDN)	2 Aug 1940	111	*Viscount Churchill*	(PDN)
15 April 1940	5039	*Rhuddlan Castle*	(PDN)	5 Aug 1940	5962	*Wantage Hall*	(PDN)
16 April 1940	4981	*Abberley Hall*	(PDN)	6 Aug 1940	4917	*Crosswood Hall*	(TYS)
17 April 1940	4960	*Pyle Hall*	(TYS)	7 Aug 1940	4082	*Windsor Castle*	(PDN)
10 May 1940	4032	*Queen Alexandra*	(LA)	8 Aug 1940	4917	*Crosswood Hall*	(TYS)
22 May 1940	111	*Viscount Churchill*	(PDN)	9 Aug 1940	5039	*Rhuddlan Castle*	(PDN)
23 May 1940	4073	*Caerphilly Castle*	(PDN)	12 Aug 1940	4959	*Purley Hall*	(SRD)
29 May 1940	5079	*Lydford Castle*	(PDN)	13 Aug 1940	6842	*Nunhold Grange*	(BL)
3 June 1940	5085	*Evesham Abbey*	(PDN)	14 Aug 1940	4082	*Windsor Castle*	(PDN)
6 June 1940	5004	*Llanstephan Castle*	(PDN)	15 Aug 1940	5023	*Brecon Castle*	(PDN)
12 June 1940	5035	*Coity Castle*	(PDN)	16 Aug 1940	5036	*Lyonshall Castle*	(PDN)
1 July 1940	5959	*Mawley Hall*	(RDG)	19 Aug 1940	6862	*Derwent Grange*	(OXY)
2 July 1940	6859	*Yiewsley Grange*	(BL)	20 Aug 1940	5085	*Evesham Abbey*	(PDN)
3 July 1940	4982	*Acton Hall*	(LDR)	21 Aug 1940	4049	*Princess Maud*	(WOS)
4 July 1940	5022	*Wigmore Castle*	(PDN)	22 Aug 1940	100A1	*Lloyds*	(PDN)
5 July 1940	4037	*The South Wales Borderers*	(PDN)	23 Aug 1940	5038	*Morlais Castle*	(PDN)
8 July 1940	5940	*Whitbourne Hall*	(PDN)	26 Aug 1940	5941	*Campion Hall*	(PDN)
9 July 1940	6858	*Woolston Grange*	(TYS)	27 Aug 1940	4917	*Crosswood Hall*	(TYS)
10 July 1940	5045	*Earl of Dudley*	(PDN)	28 Aug 1940	5015	*Kingswear Castle*	(SLP)
11 July 1940	4924	*Eydon Hall*	(TYS)	29 Aug 1940	4917	*Crosswood Hall*	(TYS)
12 July 1940	5995	*Wick Hall*	(SRD)	30 Aug 1940	5043	*Earl of Mount Edgcumbe*	(PDN)
15 July 1940	5036	*Lyonshall Castle*	(PDN)	2 Sept 1940	4987	*Brockley Hall*	(OXY)
16 July 1940	5056	*Earl of Powis*	(PDN)	3 Sept 1940	5062	*Earl of Shaftsbury*	(NA)
17 July 1940	5029	*Nunney Castle*	(PDN)	4 Sept 1940	4907	*Broughton Hall*	(PDN)
18 July 1940	4959	*Purley Hall*	(SRD)	5 Sept 1940	5069	*Isambard Kingdom Brunel*	(PDN)
19 July 1940	5036	*Lyonshall Castle*	(PDN)	6 Sept 1940	4987	*Brockley Hall*	(OXY)
22 July 1940	5987	*Brocket Hall*	(PDN)	9 Sept 1940	5920	*Wycliffe Hall*	(OXY)
23 July1940	4073	*Caerphilly Castle*	(PDN)	10 Sept 1940	4987	*Brockley Hall*	(OXY)
24 July 1940	4037	*The South Wales Borderers*	(PDN)	11 Sept 1940	5044	*Earl of Dunraven*	(PDN)
25 July 1940	4031	*Queen Mary*	(SRD)	12 Sept 1940	4075	*Cardiff Castle*	(PDN)
26 July 1940	5036	*Lyonshall Castle*	(PDN)	16 Sept 1940	4934	*Hindlip Hall*	(TYS)
29 July 1940	5945	*Leckhampton Hall*	(SRD)	17 Sept 1940	5035	*Coity Castle*	(PDN)
30 July1940	5029	*Nunney Castle*	(PDN)	18 Sept 1940	5031	*Totnes Castle*	(SRD)
31 July 1940	5004	*Llanstephan Castle*	(PDN)				

With the carpet factories going over to munitions production by 1942 the Carpet goods train was discontinued and replaced by a local class F goods to Worcester departing from Kidderminster at 8.12 pm. This was worked by a Kidderminster engine departing light from Worcester at 10.00 pm and finally arriving back at Kidderminster at 12.10 am.

On 24 July 1948 this train was worked by 4605 (TYS)

Manchester Vegetable Train   Class C

8.35pm Worcester to Manchester
Kidderminster arrive 9.3pm, depart 9.28pm.

12 April 1945	7303 (GLO)	29 June 1945	4942 *Maindy Hall* (BL)
16 April 1945	4980 *Wrottesley Hall* (WOS)	2 July 1945	4933 *Himley Hall* (PPRD)
17 April 1945	5936 *Oakley Hall* (PDN)	3 July 1945	6809 *Burghclere Grange* (PDN)
19 April 1945	6877 *Llanfair Grange* (WOS)	4 July 1945	6858 *Woolston Grange* (TYS)
17 May 1945	3835 (OXY)	5 July 1945	5977 *Beckford Hall* (PPRD)
18 May 1945	6862 *Derwent Grange* (OXY)	6 July 1945	5962 *Wantage Hall* (PDN)
24 May 1945	7317 (OXY)	9 July 1945	6943 (un-named) (WOS)
30 May 1945	6807 *Birchwood Grange* (WOS)	10 July 1945	6942 (un-named) (OXY)
4 June 1945	6930 (un-named) (WOS)	11 July 1945	4948 *Northwick Hall* (BL)
6 June 1945	5975 *Winslow Hall* (GLO)	12 July 1945	6848 *Toddington Grange* (SRD)
7 June 1945	5917 *Westminster Hall* (WOS)	16 July 1945	5365 (CNYD)
11 June 1945	5914 *Ripon Hall* (WOS)	17 July 1945	5969 *Honington Hall* (WEY)
12 June 1945	5949 *Trematon Hall* (BL)	19 July 1945	6319 (LA)
13 June 1945	5930 *Hannington Hall* (BAN)	20 July 1945	5966 *Ashford Hall* (CHR)
14 June 1945	4927 *Farnborough Hall* (BL)	23 July 1945	4926 *Fairleigh Hall* (WES)
15 June 1945	6879 *Overton Grange* (OXY)	24 July 1945	4985 *Allesley Hall* (PDN)
18 June 1945	6916 (un-named) (WOS)	26 July 1945	6874 *Haughton Grange* (NPT)
20 June 1945	5923 *Colston Hall* (CHR)	27 July 1945	6968 (un-named) (PDN)
25 June 1945	4916 *Crumlin Hall* (OXY)	29 July 1945	6817 *Gwenddwr Grange* (CDF)
26 June 1945	6806 *Blackwell Grange* (LDR)	30 July 1945	6932 (un-named) (OXY)
28 June 1945	6916 (un-named) (WOS)	31 July 1945	6865 *Hopton Grange* (PDN)

During the late 1940s this train was regularly worked by Worcester Halls 5914, 5917, 6930, 6936, 6938 and Granges 6807, 6851, 6877. Occasionally there was an exception :

20 June 1947	5949 *Trematon Hall* (BL)
3 July 1949	7801 *Anthony Manor* (SPM)
4 May 1949	6855 *Saighton Grange* (TYS)
28 May 1949	6958 *Oxburgh Hall* (SPM)
15 October 1949	2981 *Ivanhoe* (BAN)

4.40 pm Littleton & Badsey to Crewe   Class C

This fully fitted train ran as required during the fruit season. Passing time through Kidderminster 6.40 pm.

18 August 1947	3843 (RDG)	5 July 1948	5923 *Colston Hall* (CHR)
19 August 1947	5242 (NEA)	23 June 1949	3382 (WOS)
20 August 1947	7318 (RDG)	24 June 1949	3382 (WOS)
21 August 1947	5356 (RDG)	28 June 1949	2820 (CDF)
25 August 1947	6363 (RDG)	29 June 1949	5396 (SDN)
26 August 1947	5300 (OXY)	30 June 1949	2873 (EXE)
27 August 1947	2842 (NPT)		
28 August 1947	4996 *Eden Hall* (OXY)		
1 Sept 1947	6924 *Grantley Hall* (SRD)		
2 Sept 1947	3807 (BAN)		
3 Sept 1947	2883 (CHR)		

Kidderminster to Market Drayton Pools   Class H

Each morning at 10.50 am during the late 1940s a train of empty wagons departed from Kidderminster yard for Market Drayton, the locomotive arriving light from Worcester.

17 October 1947	5921 *Bingley Hall* (OXY)	25 October 1947	5927 *Guild Hall* (SRD)
21 November 1947	3448 *Kingfisher* (DID)		
3 July 1948	7403 (CNYD)	2 October 1948	3044 (CDF)
9 October 1948	6390 (BAN)	16 October 1948	WD 77393 (RDG)
13 November 1948	5942 *Doldowlod Hall* (SRD)	19 November 1948	2936 *Cefntilla Court* (CDF)
20 November 1948	WD 79235 (PPRD)	27 November 1948	2864 (PPRD)
4 December 1948	6332 (STB)	11 December 1948	2801 (PPRD)
18 December 1948	5313 (OXY)	28 December 1948	2884 (STJ)
1 January 1949	6932 *Burwarton Hall* (OXY)	22 January 1949	WD 79274 (STJ)
12 February 1949	2856 (LA)	19 February 1949	6335 (OXY)
26 February 1949	2838 (STJ)	5 March 1949	WD 77040 (OXY)
12 March 1949	WD 77115 (CHR)	25 March 1949	WD 90178 (OXY)
26 March 1949	5393 (BHD)	29 March 1949	WD 77165 (OXY)
2 April 1949	5916 *Trinity Hall* (OXY)	9 April 1949	2878 (SALOP)
16 April 1949	2873 (EXE)	14 May 1949	2802 (PPRD)
21 May 1949	5309 (OXY)	28 May 1949	3020 (SRD)
4 June 1949	7207 (OXY)	11 June 1949	5380 (DID)
25 June 1949	3831 (BAN)	2 July 1949	2874 (STB)
9 July 1949	2888 (PPRD)	23 July 1949	7243 (OXY)
13 August 1949	WD 90307 (PPRD)	20 August 1949	3861 (BAN)
1 October 1949	WD 77203 (GLO)	15 October 1949	3831 (BAN)
22 October 1949	3860 (SHL)	5 November 1949	5364 (NPT)
12 November 1949	6393 (RDG)	19 November 1949	WD 77289 (SPM)
26 November 1949	2851 (NPT)	3 December 1949	4959 *Purley Hall* (TYS)
17 December 1949	7311 (OXY)		

A.J.Turley

Aberdare 2-6-0 No. 2655 in Kidderminster yard. August 1949

GOODS TRAINS

Pontypool Road Goods   Class H

Mineral trains from Pontypool Road to the Midlands were usually in the hands of 2-8-0s.

The timings during the mid 1940s were as follows :

4.35 am Pontypool Road to Bilston	Kidderminster pass 11.3 am
5.25 am Pontypool Road to Oxley Sidings	Kidderminster pass 12.5 pm
9.0 am Pontypool Road to Priestfield	Kidderminster pass 3.40 pm
5.20 pm Pontypool Road to Oxley Sidings	Kidderminster pass 12.41 am
10.30 am Stourbridge Junction to Pontypool Road	Kidderminster pass 10.50 am
12.10 pm Bilston to Pontypool Road	Kidderminster pass 2.11 pm
11.20 pm Priestfield to Pontypool Road	Kidderminster pass 2.13 am
11.30 pm Bordesley to Pontypool Road	Kidderminster pass 2.57 am

The 4.35 am from Pontypool Road to Bilston conveyed coke for the Stewart and Lloyds plant. The wagons were of high sided steel construction, branded 'Stewart and Lloyds'. The 12.10 pm from Bilston conveyed empty coke wagons.

5 May 1949	2858 (SHL)	6 May 1949	6811 *Cranbourne Grange* (CDF)
7 May 1949	2858 (SHL	11 May 1949	WD 77040 (BHD)
15 May 1949	WD 77289 (SPM)	20 May 1949	4934 *Hindlip Hall* (LMTN)
21 May 1949	2862 (PPRD) , WD90694 (PPRD)		
27 May 1949	WD 90292 (LA)	29 May 1949	5361 (BAN) , 3862 (PPRD)
30 May 1949	5989 *Cransley Hall* (OXY	3 June 1949	WD 77001 (NA)
4 June 1949	2895 (OXY)	7 June 1949	WD 90143 (BHD)
9 June 1949	2852 (STB)	11 June 1949	3854 (SHL) , 3824 (CDF)
25 June 1949	2874 (STB)	1 July 1949	2888 (PPRD)
14 July 1949	3827 (STB)	23 July 1949	2863 (BAN) , WD 77099 (PPRD)
17 Aug 1949	WD 77380 (PPRD)	20 Aug 1949	2864 (PPRD)
25 Aug 1949	6335 (OXY)	29 Aug 1949	7240 (WOS)
2 Sept 1949	2206 (TYS)	24 Sept 1949	5963 *Wimpole Hall* (CARM)
25 Sept 1949	3816 (NPT)	26 Sept 1949	2801 (PPRD)
30 Sept 1949	WD 79232 (GLO)		
1 Oct 1949	2823 (ABDR) , 2862 (PPRD) , 3831 (BAN)		
5 Oct 1949	2898 (BAN)	7 Oct 1949	3020 (SRD)
8 Oct 1949	2884 (STJ)	10 Oct 1949	6369 (WES)
15 Oct 1949	2885 (STB) , 2888 (PPRD)	17 Oct 1949	9318 (RDG)
21 Oct 1949	5382 (CDF)	22 Oct 1949	2816 (BAN) , 3012 (PPRD)
24 Oct 1949	3022 (WOS)	12 Nov 1949	3023 (PPRD)
18 Nov 1949	6380 (CHR)	10 Dec 1949	6325 (SHL)
17 Dec 1949	5313 (OXY)		

GOODS TRAINS

Peter F. Curtis

2-8-0 T 4213 (LLY) on a Pontypool Road goods   August 1947

9.15 pm Llandilo to Stourbridge Junc. Class D
Kidderminster 5.15 am

In 1948 Stourbridge received two Grange Class 4-6-0s, 6828 *Trellech Grange* and 6857 *Tudor Grange*. These worked an overnight express Class C goods to Llandilo passing through Kidderminster at about 1.0 am. The return working was a Class D goods departing from Llandilo at 9.15 pm to Stourbridge Junction.

Some early morning observations of the northbound working are here :

2 May 1949	3851 (LLY)	14 May 1949	WD 90297 (LLY)
25 May 1949	6828 *Trellech Grange* (STB)	16 June 1949	6824 *Ashley Grange* (LLY)
24 June 1949	3807 (NPT)	25 June 1949	6862 *Derwent Grange* (OXY)
8 July 1949	2855 (LLY)	9 July 1949	6857 *Tudor Grange* (STB)
27 July 1949	6828 *Trellech Grange* (STB)		
11 August 1949	5300 (STB)	12 August 1949	5239 (NEA)
20 August 1949	5300 (STB)	29 Sept 1949	2832 (OXY)
4 Nov 1949	6828 *Trellech Grange* (STB)		

GOODS TRAINS

9.55 pm Cardiff to Oxley Sidings Class F
Kidderminster 6.35 am

22 June 1949	2830 (OXY)	24 June 1949	3826 (PPRD)	29 June 1949	2847 (PPRD)
30 June 1949	2895 (OXY)	1 July 1949	2830 (OXY)	9 July 1949	2891 (CDF)
13 July 1949	6361 (OXY)	14 July 1949	2891 (CDF)	19 July 1949	5307 (CDF)
20 July 1949	2861 (STJ)	21 July 1949	4303 (PPRD)	22 July 1949	9312 (OXY)
23 July 1949	3831 (BAN)	20 August 1949	2890 (CDF)	23 August 1949	3823 (CDF)
5 Nov 1949	7243 (OXY)	12 Nov 1949	3823 (CDF)	26 Nov 1949	2825 (OXY)

9.25 am Stourbridge Junc. to Cardiff   Class H
Kidderminster 9.50 am

14 May 1949	2887 (STJ)	28 May 1949	WD 77015 (PDN)
7 June 1949	WD 77077 (TN)	25 June 1949	2841 (SDN)
8 October 1949	4972 *Saint Brides Hall* (LA)	15 October 1949	6388 (SHL)
5 Nov 1949	3183 (STJ)	10 Dec 1949	5948 *Siddington Hall* (SPM)
17 Dec 1949	6842 *Nunhold Grange* (SPM)		

2.25 am Didcot to Kingswinford   Class F
Kidderminster 8.33 am

22 Jan 1949	WD 70843 (DID)	26 Feb 1949	6379 (DID)
19 March 1949	9308 (PDN)	26 March 1949	5381 (DID)
9 April 1949	4991 *Cobham Hall* (OXY)	16 April 1949	5985 *Mostyn Hall* (WES)
7 May 1949	WD 70843 (DID)	14 May 1949	WD 77116 (SPM)
21 May 1949	4944 *Middleton Hall* (OXY)	28 May 1949	6929 *Whorlton Hall* (BAN)
4 June 1949	WD 90201 (OXY)	11 June 1949	3859 (SHL)
18 June 1949	5945 *Leckhampton Hall* (OXY)	25 June 1949	2802 (PPRD)
2 July 1949	WD 90701 (SPM)	9 July 1949	6383 (RDG)
23 July 1949	9301 (SHL)	13 August 1949	3419 (DID)
24 Sept 1949	6918 *Sandon Hall* (LDR)	1 Oct 1949	6922 *Burton Hall* (SPM)
8 Oct 1949	4326 (DID)	12 Nov 1949	WD 77368 (RDG)
19 Nov 1949	2861 (SHL)	26 Nov 1949	4337 (SRD)

5.0 am Basingstoke to Oxley Sidings   Class F
Kidderminster 12.20 pm

7 May 1949	6312 (RDG)	14 May 1949	2875 (LA)
21 May 1949	6312 (RDG)	28 May 1949	WD 77027 (CDF)
4 June 1949	3033 (OXY)	18 June 1949	9310 (SHL)
25 June 1949	WD 77099 (PPRD)	9 July 1949	WD 79225 (CHR)
17 July 1949	WD 90201 (OXY)	20 August 1949	3825 (CNYD)
1 October 1949	2833 (OXY)	8 October 1949	3806 (STJ)
15 October 1949	7811 *Dunley Manor* (BAN)	22 October 1949	5333 (OXY)

Peter F. Curtis

Collett 0-6-0 2250 (SDN) on a Class F goods probably to Moreton Cutting, Didcot.
0-6-0T 8726 (SRD) on loan to KDR in yard 8 May 1948.

Peter F. Curtis

2-6-0 6390 (BAN) on a northbound goods   August 1947

GOODS TRAINS

A.J.Turley
An unidentified 38XX approaching Borrington Bridge in 1949

A.J.Turley
6385 approaching Hoobrook viaduct on a Class F goods in 1949

GOODS TRAINS

Rhymney Railway 0-6-2T No 75 was a rare visitor which was noted on goods trains on 28 March and 29 March 1949. It had received an overhaul at Wolverhampton Works and was being run in on goods to Worcester.

5.45 am Swindon to Oxley Sidings   Class H
Kidderminster 1.20 / 1.37 pm

7 June 1949	WD 90143 (BHD)	1 October 1949	4060 *Princess Eugenie* (SRD) + 2256 (BAN)
8 October 1949	2895 (OXY)	15 October 1949	WD 77116 (SPM)
5 Nov 1949	3836 (NPT)	12 Nov 1949	4964 *Rodwell Hall* (TYS)

Nuffield Export Trains

In the late 1940s trains conveying Nuffield cars components became a regular feature through Kidderminster. Those noted below were returning empty to Morris Cowley from Birkenhead..

26 March 1949	WD 77203 (GLO)	7 May 1949	5390 (OXF)
20 May 1949	WD 90716 (STJ)		
23 July 1949	5390 (OXF)	14 August 1949	4955 *Plaspower Hall* (OXY)
27 September 1949	4955 *Plaspower Hall* (OXY)	1 October 1949	3857 (SHL)
13 October 1949	2881 (STJ)	16 October 1949	6829 *Burmington Grange* (NA)
23 October 1949	3811 (STJ)	5 November 1949	2803 (WES)
12 November 1949	3017 (PDN)	11 December 1949	4049 *Princess Maud* (OXF)

LOCAL GOODS
8.20 a.m Shrewsbury Coton Hill to Kidderminster
Arrive 7.00pm

Pre war this was a regular Dean Goods working. With the departure of of some of the Shrewsbury Deans for war service they were replaced by LNER J25 0-6-0s which were mainly used on Severn Valley goods during the war years.

In 1945 the J25s were superseded by new GWR Collett 0-6-0s.

2 February 1940	2348 (SALOP)	12 July 1945	LNER 536 (SALOP)
13 February 1940	LNER 257 (SALOP)	14 July 1945	2234 (SALOP)
27 February 1940	LNER 536 (SALOP)	17 July 1945	2234 (SALOP)
8 March 1940	2414 (SALOP)	1 March 1947	2228 (SALOP)
11 March 1940	LNER 2059 (SALOP)	26 April 1947	2228 (SALOP)
18 March 1940	2425 (SALOP)	11 July 1947	2235 (SALOP)
19 August 1941	* 849 (OSW)	18 October 1947	2234 (SALOP)
19 March 1945	2348 (SALOP)	24 October 1947	2229 (SALOP)
25 April 1945	LNER 2059 (SALOP)	25 October 1947	2231 (SALOP)
27 April 1945	LNER 257 (SALOP)	6 March 1948	2231 (SALOP)
28 April 1945	LNER 2059 (SALOP)	26 March 1948	2231 (SALOP)
30 April 1945	** LNER 536 (SALOP) + 2044 (KDR)	1 May 1948	2229 (SALOP)
15 May 1945	2551 (WOS)	15 May 1948	2234 (SALOP)
25 May 1945	LNER 257 (SALOP)	3 July 1948	2235 (SALOP)
27 May 1945	LNER 257 (SALOP)	24 July 1948	2235 (SALOP)
2 June 1945	LNER 2059 (SALOP)	2 October 1948	2233 (SALOP)
16 June 1945	2233 (SALOP)	4 December 1948	2235 (SALOP)
22 June 1945	2234 (SALOP)	19 February 1949	2234 (SALOP)
23 June 1945	2229 (SALOP)	7 May 1949	3217 (SALOP)

- 849 was an ex Cambrian Railway 0-6-0.

** On this date the goods arrived at Kidderminster 2 hours late due to the failure of the J25. The locomotive off the Cleobury Mortimer and Ditton Priors working went to the rescue.

During the early war years the 8.20 am goods from Shrewsbury arrived at Kidderminster at around 5.0 pm and the locomotive then shunted the coal yard for an hour or two.

The locomotive stabled at Kidderminster shed overnight, departing at 5.15 am the following morning, and ran light to Hartlebury to work the 9.30 a.m Hartlebury to Shrewsbury Coton Hill goods.

LOCAL GOODS
The Tenbury   Class J
8.36 a.m Stourbridge Junc to Hereford
12.5 p.m Hereford to Stourbridge Junc.

The Tenbury goods was a two day working by Stourbridge and Hereford sheds on alternate days. The 8.36 a.m departure from Stourbridge Junc. arrived at Kidderminster at 9.45 a.m and departed at 10.50 a.m. In the reverse direction the 12.5 p.m from Hereford arrived at Kidderminster at 10.0 p.m and departed at 11.15 p.m.

During the war years the following locomotives were regularly to be seen on this goods :

LNER Class J25s	1994, 2053, 2072 and 2076 from Hereford
	29, 1973 and 2043 from Stourbridge
Aberdare 2-6-0s	2608, 2620 and 2655 from Stourbridge
	2680 from Hereford
Dean 0-6-0s	2389 and 2513 from Stourbridge
	2349 from Hereford
Bulldog 4-4-0s	3389, 3401 and from Hereford
Collett 0-6-0s	2279 and 2281 from Stourbridge
	2286 from Hereford

Post war most of the older locomotives had either moved away or been scrapped. A few observations follow :

22 March 1947	3209 (HFD)	17 May 1947	2680 (HFD)	17 June 1947	2541 (HFD)
1 May 1948	2243 (HFD)	15 May 1948	2286 (HFD)		

At the end of September 1948 the Tenbury goods was cut back to run between Kidderminster and Hereford. Collett 0-6-0 2281 was transferred from Stourbridge to Kidderminster to work this revised service.

1 October 1948	2281 (KDR)	2 October 1948	2541 (HFD)	30 October 1948	2349 (HFD)
13 November 1948	3432 (HFD)	22 November 1948	2286 (HFD)	25 March 1949	8727 (KDR)
26 March 1949	4614 (KDR)	14 May 1949	2286 (HFD)	28 May 1949	3209 (HFD)
3 June 1949	2281 (KDR)	4 June 1949	2243 (HFD)	8 August 1949	2349 (HFD)
10 August 1949	3401 *Vancouver* (HFD)		1 September 1949	4586 (KDR)	

At the end of September 1949 the Tenbury goods was cut back further to run between Kidderminster and Woofferton only. Pannier tank 3601 was transferred from Hereford to Kidderminster to work this service in exchange for 2281.

Peter F. Curtis

L.N.E.R J.25 5723 and G.W.R 2281 on Tenbury goods. September 1946
When double headed this train split at Bewdley, the leading engine working the 'run as required' Bewdley to Newnham Bridge goods.

Peter F. Curtis

Bulldog 4-4-0 3386 on Tenbury goods. 1947

LOCAL GOODS
4.40 pm Worcester to Kidderminster Class F
Arrive 8.01 pm
10.10 pm (SX) Kidderminster to Worcester

17 March 1945	3353 *Pershore Plum* (WOS)		18 May 1945	4614 (WOS)
20 March 1945	3353 *Pershore Plum* (WOS)		19 May 1945	2458 (WOS)
21 March 1945	3453 *Seagull* (PPRD)		22 May 1945	2551 (WOS)
22 March 1945	NE 2075 (WOS)		24 May 1945	2207 (WOS)
24 March 1945	2205 (WOS)		25 May 1945	4504 (WOS)
28 March 1945	5173 (WOS)		29 May 1945	4504 (WOS)
4 April 1945	4613 (WOS)		1 June 1945	2637 (STJ)
5 April 1945	4613 (WOS)		2 June 1945	4629 (WOS)
7 April 1945	5544 (WOS)		4 June 1945	7250 (SED)
9 April 1945	2294 (WOS)		6 June 1945	6396 (WOS)
10 April 1945	4534 (WOS)		7 June 1945	6679 (SED)
11 April 1945	NE 2061 (WOS)		8 June 1945	6378 (WOS)
13 April 1945	4613 (WOS)		9 June 1945	3023 (PPRD)
14 April 1945	4641 (WOS)		11 June 1945	4629 (WOS)
16 April 1945	6396 (WOS)		12 June 1945	4586 (KDR)
17 April 1945	4546 (WOS)		13 June 1945	4641 (WOS)
18 April 1945	NE 1981 (GLO)		14 June 1945	5917 *Westminster Hall* (WOS)
19 April 1945	2290 (WOS)		15 June 1945	5917 *Westminster Hall* (WOS)
20 April 1945	4504 (WOS)		16 June 1945	7301 (WOS)
21 April 1945	4629 (WOS)		19 June 1945	3100 (NPT)
23 April 1945	4114 (WOS)		21 June 1945	2679 (WOS)
24 April 1945	2205 (WOS)		22 June 1945	4546 (WOS)
25 April 1945	2774 (WOS)		23 June 1945	4504 (WOS)
26 April 1945	4641 (WOS)		25 June 1945	6306 (WOS)
27 April 1945	NE 1981 (GLO)		26 June 1945	4504 (WOS)
28 April 1945	NE 1981 (GLO)		27 June 1945	4614 (WOS)
30 April 1945	3353 *Pershore Plum* (WOS)		28 June 1945	3396 *Natal Colony* (DID)
1 May 1945	4546 (WOS)		30 June 1945	4613 (WOS)
2 May 1945	NE 1981 (GLO)		2 July 1945	4657 (WOS)
3 May 1945	4114 (WOS)		3 July 1945	4657 (WOS)
10 May 1945	2458 (WOS)		4 July 1945	5173 (WOS)
11 May 1945	6396 (WOS)		6 July 1945	2290 (WOS)
12 May 1945	4614 (WOS)		7 July 1945	4613 (WOS)
14 May 1945	4546 (WOS)		12 July 1945	2290 (WOS)
15 May 1945	4641 (WOS)		13 July 1945	4546 (WOS)
16 May 1945	4504 (WOS)		14 July 1945	5544 (WOS)
17 May 1945	4614 (WOS)			

Unusual visitors on this train included :

1 July 1947	6650 (LMTN)		13 July 1948	6147 (SHL)
4 Nov 1948	3776 (ABG)		21 Jan 1949	3441 *Blackbird* (WOS)

The 61XX 2-6-2Ts were all allocated to the London Division and were rarely seen in this area

3441 was a recent transfer from Laira.

Stourport Slack Trips

Slack trains commenced running to Stourport Power Station in 1941. These came from LMS territory, 6.32 pm ex Great Bridge (Kidderminster pass 7.45 pm) and consisted of about 36 wagons with LMS brake vans at either end. Stourbridge were allocated two 0-6-2Ts , 6665 and 6684 for this working. Initially these trains went to Hartlebury and reversed to Stourport, returning with empties.

Later an engine was provided by Kidderminster shed for trip working between Hartlebury and Stourport. This left Kidderminster shed at 7.30 am, returned during the evening as required.

The loco was usually a pannier tank or LNER J25 0-6-0, but an 0-6-2T was frequently loaned to work this service. The following were noted :

6681 (GLO)	Oct – Nov 1943	5612 (PT)	Dec 1943
5606 (PT)	Dec 1943	6677 (SED)	Dec 1943 –Feb 1944
6639 (STJ)	Feb – May 1944	5604 (LDR)	April – June 1944
5645 (STJ)	June – July 1944	6676 (STJ)	Oct 1944
6666 (STJ)	Nov 1944	6656 (PT)	Nov 1944 – Jan 1945
6639 (STJ)	Jan – March 1945	5645 (STJ)	Feb 1945
6616 (PT)	April – May 1945	6679 (SED)	May 1945
6640 (BRY)	June – Aug 1945	6686 (PT)	June 1945
5645 (STJ)	Aug 1945	6601 (SED)	Jan – April 1946
6695 (SED)	Jan 1947		

J.Davenport / Initial Photographics

This locomotive was on loan to Kidderminster during May 1945 fo working the Stourport slack trips. It was not until 1956 that Kidderminster was officially allocated its own 0-6-2T which was 6679.

Alveley Coal Trains

The Alveley coal trains required the use of a tender engine. Kidderminster supplied an LNER J.25 0-6-0 during the war years. After the departure of the J.25s moguls were used.

The first mogul to be allocated to Kidderminster was 6306 on 2 March 1946, its stay, however, was short lived being replaced by 5303 which was transferred from Gloucester on 23 March 1946. It remained at Kidderminster until 13 January 1949 when it was replaced by 6382.

The 1947 working timetable gives its duties:

```
5.20 a.m (TFO)   6.20 a.m (TFX) light engine Kidderminster to Hartlebury
5.50 a.m (TFO)   6.50 a.m (TFX) Hartlebury to Alveley Sidings
10.45 a.m   Alveley Sidings to Hartlebury
12.30 p.m   Hartlebury to Alveley Sidings
 3.20 p.m   Alveley Sidings to Worcester
 5.35 p.m   light engine Worcester to Kidderminster
```

A.J. Turley

0-6-2T 6684 approaching Kidderminster station on a slack train in 1949.

Sugar Beet Trains

The sugar beet processing campaign usually lasted about four months , commencing mid September and finishing mid January. Kidderminster received three or four complete trains per day. Some of these trains came from as far a field as the West Country and Pembrokeshire resulting in a wide variety of locomotive types from a range of depots.

Probably the most unusual locomotive to be observed on one of these trains was on 6 November 1942 when Taff Vale Railway 0-6-2T No. 385 appeared.

A second shunting engine was needed 24 hours a day to transfer the train loads to the British Sugar factory at Foley Park.

The following were noted during the 1944 season :

Date	Loco	Date	Loco
29 September 1944	3830 (NPT)	2 November 1944	2842 (NPT)
1 October 1944	4942 *Maindy Hall* (BL)	5 November 1944	6854 *Roundhill Grange* (BAN)
3 October 1944	4978 *Westwood Hall* (PDN)		WD 7011 (OXY)
5 October 1944	6920 (un-named) (PDN)	6 November 1944	5953 *Dunley Hall* (STJ)
6 October 1944	2800 (CDF)	7 November 1944	3009 (NEY)
7 October 1944	2651 (PPRD)		6967 (un-named) (OXY)
8 October 1944	2676 (GLO)	8 November 1944	6371 (NEY)
10 October 1944	3031 (OXF)	10 November 1944	WD 7461 (WOS)
11 October 1944	2882 (BAN)	11 November 1944	2656 (GLO)
13 October 1944	WD 7461 (WOS)		5943 *Elmdon Hall* (SDN)
15 October 1944	6858 *Woolston Grange* (TYS)	12 November 1944	LMS 8441 (BL)
16 October 1944	5246 (SED)		2215 (TN)
17 October 1944	4260 (STJ)	13 November 1944	LMS 8412 (BL)
18 October 1944	NE 2061 (WOS)		2877 (CDF)
19 October 1944	NE 2075 (WOS)		3805 (NPT)
20 October 1944	2833 (BAN)	15 November 1944	WD 7489 (RDG)
21 October 1944	3026 (CHR)	17 November 1944	6399 (BAN)
	NE 2061 (WOS)		5667 (BRY)
	6319 (LA)	18 November 1944	2887 (STJ)
22 October 1944	3811 (LA)		5368 (NEY)
	6821 *Leaton Grange* (NPT)		LMS 8452 (WOS)
23 October 1944	2651 (PPRD)	19 November 1944	3830 (NPT)
25 October 1944	2256 (BAN)	22 November 1944	LMS 8442 (PDN)
26 October 1944	2873 (BL)	24 November 1944	6656 (PT)
27October 1944	2660 (LLY)	25 November 1944	6344 (CARM)
27 October 1944	LMS 8451 (WOS)	26 November 1944	2808 (ABDR)
	6676 (STJ)	28 November 1944	5332 (OXY)
28 October 1944	4272 (NEA)	8 December 1944	7207 (LLY)
	6849 *Walton Grange* (BAN)	10 December 1944	4975 *Umberslade Hall* (CDF)
29 October 1944	3803 (BAN)	16 December 1944	3036 (ABDR)
30 October 1944	WD 7047 (OXY)	17 December 1944	3031 (OXY)
	3010 (LLY)	27 December 1944	2828 (ABDR)
1 November 1944	WD 7457 (SDN)		3024 (OXY)
2 November 1944	5212 (LLY)		

STEAM- Museum of the Great Western Railway, Swindon
Taff Vale 0-6-2T No. 385
A rare visitor on a sugar beet train

Noted during the 1948 season were :

24 September 1948	5914 *Ripon Hall* (WOS)	13 November 1948	9301 (SHL)
	WD 78761 (LA)		5348 (HFD)
26 September 1948	6324 (WOS)	20 November 1948	6951 *Impney Hall* (WOS)
9 October 1948	2570 (CDF)	21 November 1948	6846 *Ruckley Grange* (SPM)
	6396 (WOS)	4 December 1948	2866 (NPT)
16 October 1948	5325 (BL)		6395 (HFD)
17 October 1948	WD 79274 (STJ)	12 December 1948	6306 (WOS)
	6324 (WOS)	27 December 1948	6396 (WOS)
30 October 1948	2207 (WOS)	28 December 1948	2881 (STJ)
	3219 (WOS)		7311 (OXY)
	7315 (SRD)	1 January 1949	2867 (LA)
1 November 1948	4128 (BHD)	9 January 1949	WD 77064 (OXY)
4 November 1948	2866 (NPT)		6382 (WOS)
12 November 194	4939 *Littleton Hall* (TYS)	16 January 1949	5303 (KDR)

Noted during the 1949 season were :

24 September 1949	WD 77326 (SPM)	30 October 1949	3861 (BAN)
30 September 1949	6362 (OXY)	31 October 1949	3859 (SHL)
1 October 1949	4904 *Binnegar Hall* (OXY)	5 November 1949	6936 *Breccles Hall* (WOS)
	6926 *Holkham Hall* (NPT)	6 November 1949	9304 (PDN)
6 October 1949	3010 (CARM)		5917 *Westminster Hall* (WOS)
7 October 1949	3033 (OXY)	10 November 1949	6379 (RDG)
	WD 77326 (SPM)	12 November 1949	6393 (RDG)
8 October 1949	WD 90297 (LLY)	13 November 1949	5987 *Brocket Hall* (PDN)
9 October 1949	3820 (BAN)		2859 (SPM)
12 October 1949	6350 (BHD)	20 November 1949	3803 (SHL)
13 October 1949	2848 (BAN)	26 November 1949	WD 77012 (BAN)
15 October 1949	3831 (BAN)	3 December 1949	WD 90524 (CDF)
22 October 1949	5905 *Knowsley Hall* (FGD)	4 December 1949	6877 *Llanfair Grange* (WOS)
	6324 (WOS)	13 December 1949	5170 (STB)
23 October 1949	WD 90715 (WOS)	25 December 1949	3031 (OXY)
			6378 (WOS)

Raw Sugar Specials

Outside the beet season train loads of cane sugar would arrive for processing at the factory. These trains came from the docks at Newport and Cardiff. Noted in 1949 were :

2 June 1949   5364 (NPT)   4 June 1949   7235 (PPRD)
25 June 1949   2931 *Arlington Court* (BL)   1 July 1949   2873 (EXE)
2 July 1949   9300 (SHL)

Trains of raw sugar for final refining from other sugar factories also came to Kidderminster, one such train was on 15 May 1949 which was handed over to the GWR at Crewe. The locomotive was 5303 (KDR).

Molasses Tanks

Train loads of Molasses tanks for Avonmouth docks departed from the sugar factory. Noted in 1949 were :

5 November 1949   6396 (WOS)
9 November 1949   6324 (WOS)
19 November 1949   9064 *Trevithick* (GLO)
30 November 1949   3214 (WOS)

Instructions for working to Sugar Beet Factory Sidings.
Appendix to Service Timetable February 1943

KIDDERMINSTER AND BEWDLEY—(Single Line).
Kidderminster (Junction) and Bewdley (South).
Sugar Beet Factory Sidings at Foley Park, situated between Kidderminster (Junction) and Bewdley (South).

1. The four Sidings adjoining the single running line at Foley Park are available for use for traffic purposes.
2. The Sidings have a connection with the running line, facing from the direction of Kidderminster; the points are worked from a ground frame locked by key on the Electric Train Token for the section Kidderminster Junction—Bewdley South. The site of the connection with the running line at the Sidings is on a short stretch of level ; the running line on the Kidderminster side to a point just before reaching the connection is on a gradient of 1 in 112, falling towards the Siding, and on the Bewdley side the line rises 1 in 115 in the direction of Bewdley.
3. An Intermediate Electric Train Token instrument is fixed in the ground frame cabin for the reception and issue of the Token for the Kidderminster Junction—Bewdley South Section. Telephonic communication with Kidderminster Junction Signal Box is provided in the ground frame cabin.
4. Traffic for and from the Sidings will be worked specially from and to Kidderminster under the following regulations :—
  (a) The trips on the forward journey will be signalled between Kidderminster Junction and Bewdley South Signal Boxes, under Electric Train Token Regulation 13, Clause (a) and must be accompanied by two men.
  (b) Trips to the Sidings must not exceed 35 wagons, engine and van (except as provided in Clause 7) and two men must accompany each trip.
  (c) The Guard of the train will be in charge of the working at the Sidings, and the Shunter will be solely responsible for dealing with the Electric Train Token at the Sidings ; all speaking communication between the Shunter and the Kidderminster Signalman must be conducted over the telephone on the Kidderminster Local circuit.

Sugar Beet Factory Sidings at Foley Park, situated between Kidderminster (Junction) and Bewdley (South)—*continued.*

(*d*) Upon arrival at Foley Park the complete train must be shunted to the Sidings ; when this has been done, and the running line is clear, the Shunter must place the Token in the instrument and advise the Kidderminster Junction Signalman on the telephone that he has done so, and that the single line is clear for the passage of trains ; when the Kidderminster Junction Signalman has received this advice he must act in accordance with Electric Train Token Regulation 13, Clause (*b*) by sending the " Shunting completed " signal 2—5 to Bewdley South. After this signal has been sent and acknowledged, the Signalmen must test the Electric Train Token instruments and if in order, other trains may pass over the single line section in the usual way whilst the train is locked in the Sidings.

(*e*) When the train is ready to leave the Sidings, the Shunter must telephone the Kidderminster Junction Signalman and ask permission to make the required movements ; if the single line is clear to the Kidderminster Junction Down branch home signal and the train can be accepted, the Shunter must be so informed ; Kidderminster Junction Signalman must send the " Release Token for shunting " code 5—2 to Bewdley South Box, and when this signal has been acknowledged, both Signalmen must depress the bell plungers on the respective Token instruments which will enable the Shunter to withdraw the Token at the Sidings, to enable him to unlock the ground frame and set the points for the train to draw on to the running line. Two indicating needles connected with the Token instrument are fixed in the ground frame, and when the Shunter attempts to obtain the Token, the needles should be deflected if both Signalmen are depressing their bell plungers.

(*f*) After the train has drawn out of the Sidings the points must be reversed and the ground frame locked ; the train may then proceed to Kidderminster Junction Branch Home signal, the Driver carrying the Token in the usual way. When handing the Token to the Driver, the Shunter must instruct him that the line is clear only to the Branch Home signal at Kidderminster Junction.

(*g*) When the train, with tail lamp attached, has arrived at Kidderminster Junction, and the Electric Token has been restored to the instrument, the " Shunting completed " signal, 2—5, must be sent to Bewdley South.

(*h*) If the train cannot be accepted when it is ready to leave the Siding, the Shunter will be so informed by the Kidderminster Junction Signalman who must advise the Shunter subsequently when the train can be accepted ; the Shunter will be responsible for reminding the Signalman when a train is waiting.

(*i*) Attention is drawn to the instructions contained on page 43 of the General Appendix to the Rule Book respecting the method to be employed when placing a Token in, and withdrawing one from, the instrument.

(*j*) If the telephone on the Kidderminster Local circuit has failed, the Shunter may use the telephone on the Tenbury Wells—Worcester Exchange circuit for the purpose of communicating with the Kidderminster Junction Signalman.

(*k*) If both telephones in the ground frame have failed, the Shunter must at once proceed on foot to Kidderminster Junction, and notify the Signalman there the position, and make arrangements, according to circumstances for a Token to be conveyed to the Sidings.

5. Trips may be run between Kidderminster and the Sidings at night during the time the branch line is closed, when the following arrangements must operate :—

(*a*) After the last booked ordinary train has passed through the Bewdley South—Kidderminster Junction Section, and before Bewdley South Signal Box closes for the night, an Electric Train Token must be withdrawn at Kidderminster Junction Box, to be used for trains requiring to run between Kidderminster and Foley Park Sidings during the time the branch is closed.

(*b*) No train must be allowed to proceed to the branch without the Token, and when the latter is handed to the Driver he must be advised of the branch line being closed, and that the train must only run to and from Foley Park Sidings upon the authority of the Token ; the train to return from the Sidings without going through the block section.

(*c*) The Driver must keep the Token in his possession the whole of the time the train is on the branch except when it is required to operate the ground frame. The Token must not on these occasions be deposited in the Electric Token instrument at the Sidings.

(*d*) Upon returning from the Sidings, the Driver must approach Kidderminster Junction cautiously and be prepared to stop at the branch home signal.

(*e*) The Token, when not in use, must be in the custody of the Signalman at Kidderminster Junction Box to whom it must be delivered immediately upon the return of each trip from the Sidings, with an assurance that the branch line is clear.

(*f*) The forward and return times of the trips must be recorded in the Kidderminster Junction train register book.

(*g*) The time the Token is withdrawn at night, and the time it is restored to the instrument in the morning, upon Bewdley South Box opening, must be recorded in the respective train register books.

6. When necessary, trips may be propelled from Kidderminster Junction to the Sidings in clear weather only, and in connection with these movements the undermentioned regulations must be observed :—

(*a*) The Driver must proceed cautiously, running at reduced speed, and keep a sharp lookout for hand signals.

(*b*) A goods brake van must be the leading vehicle ; a Guard or other competent man must ride in it, keep a sharp lookout and be prepared to exhibit any hand signals necessary to the Driver, the usual side and tail lamps being carried on the brake van. After sunset a lamp shewing a white light in the direction of Bewdley must be carried on the brake van, and the engine must carry a lamp shewing a red light to the rear.

(*c*) Upon arrival at the Sidings, before any shunting is commenced on the running line, the hand brake in the Guard's van must be screwed on tightly, and in addition, wagon brakes, if necessary, applied to securely hold the vehicles on the running line. After sunset the side and tail lamps on the brake van must be replaced, and shew red lights towards Bewdley, and the side lamps white lights towards Kidderminster.

(*d*) A brake van must always be at the Bewdley end of vehicles shunted on the running line.

(*e*) Upon returning from the Sidings the train must be drawn, the ordinary head, side and tail lamps being carried.

7. A train consisting of 60 loaded wagons may be propelled from Kidderminster Junction to Foley Park Sidings in clear weather during the hours that the branch line is closed for ordinary Passenger and Freight train services under the instructions shewn in Clauses 5 and 6, provided an additional brake van is formed in the centre of the train with a man in it equipped with the necessary lamp and flags to enable hand signals from the Guard riding in the leading van to be transmitted to the Enginemen.

Note.—If a trip, consisting of engine and brake van only, is required to run from Kidderminster Junction to the Sidings during fog or falling snow, the brake van may be propelled. When propelling is carried out, the instructions contained in paragraph 6 must be strictly observed so far as they are applicable to this movement.

8. Freight trains from the direction of Bewdley required to call at Foley Park Sidings must be dealt with in accordance with Electric Train Token Regulation 8, Clause (*f*), and upon arrival at the Sidings, before any shunting is commenced on the running line, the hand brake in the Guard's van must be screwed on tightly ; in addition wagon brakes must be applied, and, if necessary, sprags, to securely hold the vehicles on the running line.

If it is found, after arrival at the Sidings, there is insufficient time to perform the work required, and for the train to proceed to Kidderminster Junction and clear the section by the time desired, the train must be shunted clear of the Main Line at Foley Park ; when this has been done, the Shunter must place the Token in the instrument and advise the Kidderminster Junction Signalman on the telephone that he has done so, and that the single line is clear for the passage of trains ; the Kidderminster Junction Signalman will then advise the Bewdley South Signalman, both Signalmen will turn the respective indicators to " Token in," test instruments, and pass trains over the single line section in the usual way whilst the train is locked in the Sidings.

Trains from the Bewdley direction will call at the Sidings only upon prior arrangement being made with the Kidderminster Station Master, who must send a Shunter to meet the trains at the Sidings.

—————————

On 1 May 1948 an 0-4-0ST British Sugar Corporation No. 3 arrived at Kidderminster in a goods train. This was a brand new locomotive built by Andrew Barclay Sons, and Co. Ltd. (works no. 2248/48) at their Caledonia works in Kilmarnock. This was an addition to the existing locomotives at the factory, Nos 1 and 2, both Andrew Barclay 0-4-0 Saddle Tanks.

A. Norman H. Glover

British Sugar Corporation No.3

FOLEY PARK

Kidderminster Railway Museum / W.Potter

Foley Park Halt with British Sugar factory sidings on the right.

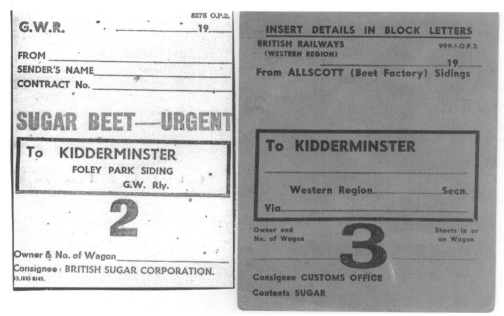

Wagon labels for traffic bound for Foley Park.

SMETHWICK DROP FORGINGS LTD. (M.O.S)

Additional track work was laid down in the early part of the war to enable the S.D.F factory to be accessed by rail via the sugar factory sidings. The amount of traffic warranted the S.D.F to be supplied with their own locomotive 0-4-0ST 'S.D.F No. 1' built by William Barclay of Stafford in 1942. Works No. 2664/42. It remained at Foley Park until 1947.

Other Perishable Traffic

Between late autumn and early summer broccoli and potato specials ran from Cornwall. To handle this traffic locomotives from other divisions were loaned to Cornish sheds which explains the wide variety of sheds noted on these trains.

Potato Specials

3 June 1949	3821 (STB)	9 June 1949	WD 77241 (NA)
	WD 90642 (LA)		WD 79234 (PDN)
4 June 1949	WD 90212 (LA)	11 June 1949	5355 (PPRD)
	2893 (NPT)		WD 77077 (TN)
5 June 1949	6832 *Brockton Grange* (BAN)	13 June 1949	3807 (NPT)
7 June 1949	4976 *Warfield Hall* (CHR)	14 June 1949	4976 *Warfield Hall* (CHR)
	WD 77102 (NPT)		2894 (NPT)
	3803 (SHL)		7307 (OXY)
		17 June 1949	5370 (TYS)

Broccoli Specials

Broccoli specials ran from Marazion to Oxley Sidings, some continuing to Crewe or Saltney. Cattle trucks (suitably cleaned) were used on these trains.

12 December 1948	4969 *Shrugborough Hall* (SPM)		
20 February 1949	2833 (OXY)	27 March 1949	5360 (SHL)
27 February 1949	3856 (SHL)	3 April 1949	4960 *Pyle Hall* (SRD)
	6876 *Kingsland Grange* (SPM)		6399 (WES)
6 March 1949	6321 (SRD)	10 April 1949	3823 (CDF)
19 March 1949	3803 (SHL)		5987 *Brockley Hall* (PDN)
20 March 1949	2844 (SPM)		
	6863 *Dolhywel Grange* (SPM)		

Banana Specials

Banana specials were class C goods from Avonmouth Docks probably en route to Birmingham

11 November 1948	4991 *Cobham Hall* (OXY)	14 February 1949	3808 (STJ)
25 March 1948	6384 (SDN)	7 July 1949	6820 *Kingstone Grange* (NPT)
21 July 1949	3831 (BAN)		

Meat Specials

4 December 1948	4377 (WES)

Ballast and Permanent Way Trains

Ballast trains were of particular interest, especially those from the GWR quarries at Llynclys, near Oswestry, which usually would have a locomotive from Oswestry shed – quite rare at Kidderminster.

26 September 1948	4-4-0 Dukedog 9028 (OSW)	from Llynclys Junc.
13 April 1949	4-4-0 Dukedog 9003 (OSW)	from Llynclys Jumc.
22 May 1949	4977 *Whatcombe Hall* (GLO)	from Chepstow
18 June 1949	7303 (CHEL)	from Chepstow
14 July 1949	2-6-2T 8103 (OSW)	from Llynclys Junc.
26 September 1949	2-6-2T 8103 (OSW)	from Llynclys Junc.

Other Permanent Way and Breakdown trains included :

23 March 1947	2231 (SRD)	breakdown train.
15 June 1947	6391 (SRD)	Wolverhampton breakdown crane.
6 September 1947	4504 (WOS)	breakdown train. Railcar No. 7 derailed leaving Yew Tree Road siding.
30 October 1948	2263 (WOS)	breakdown train. 6 sugar beet wagons and brake van derailed.
12 December 1948	Railcar No. 33 (STB)	with tunnel inspection wagon.
13 March 1949	6391 (SRD)	with engineer's inspection coach.
3 April 1949	4121 (BHD)	
10 August 1949	5958 *Knolton Hall* (CDF)	with engineer's inspection coach.
22 September 1949	7222 (WOS)	
13 October 1949	7315 (SRD)	with engineer's inspection coach.
13 November 1949	3382 (WOS)	
19 November 1949	6138 (OXF)	breakdown train. Wagons derailed.
30 November 1949	2290 (WOS)	4678 (HFD), on loan to KDR, derailed in yard.
19 December 1949	3029 (WOS)	train load of sleepers to Kidderminster.

Loco Coal Trains   Class H

Train loads of locomotive coal ran from Aberdare to Stourbridge and Wolverhampton. The coal was conveyed in steel bodied 20 ton wagons branded 'LOCO'. The locomotives were usually 2-8-0s.

26 March 1949	WD 90716 (STJ)	14 May 1949	2821 (CDF)
7 May 1949	2897 (BAN)	27 May 1949	WD 90631 (BAN)
28 May 1949	WD 90694 (PPRD)	3 June 1949	2883 (BAN)
4 June 1949	2885 (STB)	10 June 1949	2854 (LMTN)
2 July 1949	6667 (STB)	13 August 1949	3850 (STJ)
28 August 1949	2820 (CDF)	21 October 1949	2892 (STJ)
22 October 1949	2874 (STB)	12 November 1949	2876 (NPT)

Cattle Trains

Cattle trains were run on market days as required to Bordesley.

From Worcester Butts Siding on Mondays   (Kidderminster 6.27 pm)
    Tenbury on alternate Tuesdays   (Kidderminster 7.15 pm)
    Bridgnorth on alternate Mondays   (Kidderminster 7.15pm)
    Hereford on Wednesdays   (Kidderminster 7.37 pm)

These did not usually produce any locomotives of great interest but on 26 May 1943 Cambrian Railway 0-6-0 887 (OSW) was noted on the Hereford cattle train.

8793 (GLO) was noted on a special cattle train on Friday 23 May 1947. It was unusual to see a pannier tank on a cattle train. The usual motive power was an 0-6-0 tender engine.

2279 (STB) was noted on Thursday 26 May 1949 with a loaded cattle train at 8.30 pm. Heading towards Stourbridge.

Empty Cattle Trains Bordesley Junc. / Oxley Sidings to Fishguard Harbour
Class D

Date	Locomotive	Time
9 January 1949	2249 (OXF)	
29 March 1949	6807 *Birchwood Grange* (WOS)	
31 May 1949	2823 (OXY)	7.15 pm
7 July 1949	2846 (SPM)	6.50 pm
11 July 1949	2953 *Titley Court* (CHR)	6.55 pm

H.C Casserley

Cambrian Railway 0-6-0 887 at Moat Lane in 1948
This locomotive was noted at Kidderminster on a Hereford cattle train
On 26 May 1943

Kidderminster Shunting Engines

Extracts from the Service Timetable commencing 7th October 1946 :

ENGINE No.1
    Start 6.0 am Monday morning
    Sunt Yard, etc., trip to Foley Park 9.5 am. And trip Bewdley to Kidderminster, 12.50 pm.
    Trip to Whitehouse's siding 2.0 pm, and trip to Foley Park 5.0 pm. Engine changed daily at 1.0 pm.
    To shed 2.0 pm Sunday.

ENGINE No. 2
    Start 4.0 pm.
    Shunts New Coal Yard and Mileage Sidings. To shed 12.0 midnight. Engine out continuously during
    Beet Season.

In 1940 the regular yard shunter was 0-6-0 pannier tank 8727. The evening Coal Yard shunter was usually a Shrewsbury 0-6-0 tender engine which had worked the goods down the Severn Valley. From the mid 1940s the Coal Yard shunting was performed by any available Kidderminster engine.

The main shunting engine was provided with a shunting truck.

During a break in shunting operations at about 8.0 pm the engine and truck, carrying most of the shunters, would go up to the buffer stops at the Station Hill end and the men would visit the 'Railway Bell Hotel'!

In September 1942 Kidderminster received a brand new pannier tank No 4625 from Swindon. 3609 was also transferred to Kidderminster during that year, making a total of four 57XX to choose from. 8718 was the usual Stourport shunting engine.

3609 was involved in a collision in Kidderminster yard in October 1944 and was replaced by 7700 transferred from Gloucester.

Kidderminster Railway Museum
Group of shunters and footplate crew.
Locomotive 0-6-0T 4641 and shunting truck No. 41098.

Kidderminster Yard Shunting Engines

Peter F.Curtis

4625 at work April 1948

Peter F. Curtis

8727 outside outside shunters' cabin July 1947

Kidderminster Shunting Truck.

By riding on a shunting truck shunters were able to move around the yard in greater safety than by riding on the locomotive footsteps,

A shunting truck had a large toolbox containing spare lamps, shunting poles, brake sticks, sprags and re-railers.

The Kidderminster shunting truck was No. 41098 built in 1938 to diagram M4. It was transferred to Kidderminster during the early part of the war, replacing No. 41803 which was built in 1901.

Shunting Horses.

Locomotives were prohibited from entering the goods shed. The GWR employed two horses which were accommodated in a four berth stable located on the other side of the main line to the goods shed, behind the carriage sidings. One horse was used per day which had to be led across the tracks. Two men would be required during the shunting operation, one to look after the horse and the other to be in charge of the wagons.

Messrs Harvey & Co. also employed a horse to move wagons around their private siding.

P.F.Curtis

View of Kidderminster Junction Signal Box taken from the Wooden Bridge.
Signal Box built 1938, demolished by derailed goods train on 4 June 1953.

Light Engine Workings

On Sunday evenings during 1945 there were light engine workings from Worcester to Stourbridge / Wolverhampton sheds for working goods trains the following day.

Sunday 25 March 1945	6371 (NEY) + 2673 (NPT) + LMS 8458 (OXY)
Sunday 8 April 1945	3208 (SRD) + 6835 *Eastham Grange* (BAN)
Sunday 15 April 1945	5335 (CDF) + 6377 (STJ) + 2831 (ABDR)
Sunday 22 April 1945	2802 (ABDR) + 7306 (NEY)
Sunday 6 May 1945	2801 (ABDR) + 2651 (PPRD) +3041 (SPM)
Sunday 13 May 1945	2825 (OXY) 6843 *Poulton Grange* (TYS) + 2623 (OXY) + 3030 (WOS)
Sunday 20 May 1945	2829 STJ) + 2817 (BAN) + 5316 (BHD)
Sunday 27 May 1945	LMS 8407 (NA) + LMS 8438 (PDN) 4965 *Rood Ashton Hall* (BL) 3863 (BL) + 3808 (CDF) + 2636 (NPT)
Sunday 10 June 1945	5927 *Guild Hall* (SRD) + mogul
Sunday 17 June 1945	LMS 8425 (EXE) + 3847 (OXF) 2637 (STJ) + LMS 8466 (STJ)
Sunday 1 July 1945	3845 (RDG) 2832 (ABDR) + 7200 (NA)
Sunday 8 July 1945	5379 (OXY) + 3002 (PPRD) 2804 (CDF) + LMS 8462 (NPT)
Sunday 15 July 1945	2821 (CDF) + 2813 (PPRD) + 2800 (CDF) 2874 (CDF) + 4946 *Moseley Hall* (PZ)
Sunday 22 July 1945	2888 (BAN)
Sunday 12 August 1945	3030 (WOS) + 28xx LMS 8453 (NPT) + 3017 (BL) + LMS 8426 (OXY)
Sunday 19 August 1945	6906 *Chicheley Hall* (BAN) + 2846 (BL) 3840 (RDG) + 7208 LLY) + 3862 (OXF) 5989 *Cransley Hall* (OXY) + 3013 (BL)
Sunday 26 August 1945	5300 (OXY) + 3005 (TYS) + 2879 (NPT)
Sunday 12 Sept 1945	3216 (OSW) + LMS 8460 (OXY) LMS 8463 (CDF) LMS 8474 (OXY) + 3831 (NPT)

Light Engine Workings

Other light engine workings of note included small South Wales tanks en route to /from Wolverhampton Stafford Road Works. These workings caused great excitement among the local enthusiasts because they produced shunting engines which rarely worked far from their home shed.

		class				class	
2 April 1940	6748 (BRY)	57XX	0-6-0T	24 April 1940	2722 (NEA)	27XX	0-6-0T
14 June 1940	5818 (PPRD)	58XX	0-4-2T	7 August 1940	7720 (PPRD	57XX	0-6-0T
8 August 1940	5714 (STJ)	57XX	0-6-0T	28 August 1941	2113 (PILL)	2021	0-6-0T
9 Sept 1941	2047 (CARM)	2021	0-6-0T	16 Sept 1941	1996 (WTD)	850	0-6-0T
16 Sept 1941	2037 (PPRD)	2021	0-6-0T	15 Feb 1942	8778 (TDU	57XX	0-6-0T
12 April 1942	2115 (GLO)	2021	0-6-0T	14 April 1942	2734 (PILL)	2721	0-6-0T
19 July 1944	5778 (NEA)	57XX	0-6-0T	29 August 1944	3690 (NPT)	57XX	0-6-0T
9 June 1945	3747 (ABDR)	57XX	0-6-0T	12 January 1947	5697 (PT)	56XX	0-6-2T
18 Feb 1947	1745 (PT)	655	0-6-0T	10 June 1947	5768 (PPRD)	57XX	0-6-0T
1 Sept 1947	2063 (NPT)	2021	0-6-0T	17 Dec 1947	1888 (CED)	1854	0-6-0T
17 April 1948	6687 (PPRD)	56XX	0-6-2T	25 Sept 1948	6428 (NPT)	64XX	0-6-0T
8 Jan 1949	4668 (PPRD)	57XX	0-6-0T	14 May 1949	8702 (SPM)	57XX	0-6-0T
24 July 1949	4515 (WTD)	45XX	2-6-2T	2 Sept 1949	5693 (BRY)	56XX	0-6-2T
8 Sept 1949	5619 (AYN)	56XX	0-6-2T				

The 655, 850 and 1854 classes noted were all of 1890s vintage.

Light engines were also to be seen en route to Worcester or Swindon works.

		class				class	
17 Nov 1948	2095 (SRD)	2021	0-6-0T	1 Jan 1949	1863 (SRD)	1854	0-6-0T
2 Sept 1949	4512 (MCH)	45XX	2-6-2T	8 Nov 1949	4560 (MCH)	45XX	2-6-2T

War Department and U.S Army locomotives were occasionally to be seen running light engine between Depots.

April 1942	WD 84 (ex LNER Class J69 0-6-0T) en route from Melbourne to Long Marston
14 January 1943	WD 175 (ex GW Dean Goods 2511) Wolverhampton Works to Canterbury West
25 February 1944	1942 U.S.A 0-6-0T Worcester Works to Melbourne Military Railway
14 June 1944	1407 U.S.A 0-6-0T Melbourne Military Railway to Newport Ebbw Junc. prior to Shipment to the Continent.
27 April 1946	WD 70095 (ex GW Dean Goods 2470) Bicester to Shopshire & Montgomery Rly.

On 12 June 1944 U.S.A 0-4-0 Petrol locomotives Nos. 7770, 7771 and 7772 were seen in an up goods train en route to Southampton.

The following Bulldogs were noted travelling towards Worcester running light, being transferred from Laira to Worcester Division Sheds. 3445 and 3446 were both withdrawn before the end of the year.

1 August 1948   3401 Vancouver (LA) + 3446 Goldfinch (LA)

2 August 1948   3445 Flamingo (LA)

MILITARY
&
GOVERNMENT TRAFFIC

CIVILIAN EVACUATION TRAINS

On 2 June 1940 there were a number of trains evacuating children from the Eastern Counties. One such train arrived at Kidderminster from Clacton after an 8 hour journey. The route taken was via Ipswich, Cambridge, Oxford and Worcester.

In the summer of 1944 trains arrived at Kidderminster from the London area with families to avoid the V-Bombs.

2.40 pm   Sunday 20 August 1944 bringing 57 women and 133 children.

Tuesday 29 August 1944 bringing 69 women and 155 children.

HOSPITAL TRAINS

Following D-Day 1944 hospital/ambulance trains were frequently to be seen at Kidderminster. The British ones were mainly from Shrivenham en route to Tettenhall or Wombourne. The American ones brought casualties from ports and airfields in the south of England to Kidderminster and Stourport for the local U.S hospitals. Other U.S trains passed through Kidderminster en route to U.S hospitals in north Shropshire. Trains with U.S casualties for repatriation to the U.S.A also came through Kidderminster en route from Malvern Wells to Liverpool or Glasgow.

The unloading at Kidderminster was done at one of the sidings adjacent to the goods shed, access to which was via the down goods loop. Local enthusiasts knew in advance when a train was due because all the points over which the train was to pass were clamped. Armed guards protected the train while it was being unloaded. Even engine crew going off duty from KDR shed via the goods yard were often challenged.

There were 3 types of Ambulance Trains, or Hospital Trains as the U.S Army called them, in operation in the U.K.

(a)   Overseas Ambulance Train (O.A.T.) which were Westinghouse Air braked. Each train was hauled throughout its journey by an LNER Westinghouse braked 4-6-0 locomotive Class B.12/3 with a permanent crew consisting of 2 Drivers, 2 Firemen, 1 Fitter and 2 Guards. These trains were for the use of the U.S Army and were destined for use on the Continent. Train No. 11-15, 17, 27, 31, 33, 36 and 37.

(b)   Home Ambulance Train (H.A.T.) which were vacuum braked. 7 trains were for the use of the British Army (Nos. 56, 58, 60, 62, 63, 65 and 66). 5 trains were allocated for the U.S Army (Nos. 55, 57, 59, 61 and 64).

In November 1944 two Improvised Home Ambulance Trains were brought into service to replace O.A.Ts sent to the Continent.

In February 1945 six further H.A.Ts entered service Nos. 67-72

(c)   Casualty Evacuation Train (C.E.T.) which were vacuum braked. Unlike the O.A.Ts and H.A.Ts these trains had minimal medical facilities on board and were mainly used on short trips.

U.S Hospital Trains to Kidderminster

Date	Train No.	Locomotive	Entraining station	Patients
11 June 1944	H12	LNER 8518 + GWR 7308	Netley	316
13 June 1944			Winchester	226
15 June 1944			Axminster	277
22 June 1944	H15	LNER 8557	Chiseldon	306
6 July 1944		GWR 7320 (RDG)		250
14 July 1944				268
23 July 1944	H27	LNER 8509 + GWR 6306		315
25 July 1944	H14	LNER 8525	Swindon	291
5 August 1944	H14	LNER 8525	Newbury	268
14 August 1944	H33	LNER 8554		284
3 September 1944	H13	LNER 8519		291
29 September 1944	H11	LNER 8547		292

Date	Train No.	Locomotive	Entraining station	Patients
October 1944				
24 October 1944		LNER		292
November 1944				
10 November 1944		LNER 8530		
December 1944				
December 1944				
18 December 1944	H2		Netley	320
December 1944				

There were 20 hospital train arrivals at Kidderminster during 1944 with casualties for the U.S 52nd General Hospital at Wolverley. Records for 1945 are rather more sketchy, but there were probably a further dozen before the closure of the hospital in August 1945.

Recorded arrivals in 1945 were :

Date	Locomotive(s)
15 April 1945	6365 (FGD) ex Swindon Works
21 April 1945	5367 (SDN) + 5134 (STB)
10 May 1945	
6 June 1945	

Doris McKenzie-Keselowski

Unloading U.S casualties in Kidderminster goods yard 1944.

88

Doris McKenzie-Keselowsky

Unloading U.S casualties in Kidderminster goods yard
1944

Doris McKenzie-Keselowsky

U.S Army Ambulances lining up in Kidderminster goods yard

Rex Conway collection

LNER Class B12/3 No. 8516
This locomotive came to Kidderminster and Stourport on Hospital Trains.

U.S Hospital Trains to Stourport

Locomotives on the hospital trains to Stourport were serviced at Kidderminster shed and turned on the Bewdley / Kidderminster / Hartlebury triangle.

Date	Train No.	Locomotive	Entraining station	Patients
19 July 1944	H11	LNER 8516	Axminster	292
23 July 1944	H14	LNER 8525	Swindon	292
28 July 1944	H12	LNER 8518		292
2 August 1944	H17	LNER 8555		304
15 August 1944	H14	LNER 8525	Netley	292
20 September 1944	H14		Netley	292
5 October 1944				292
16 October 1944				296
24 October 1944	H14		Chiseldon	292
26 October 1944			Southampton	292
7 November 1944				292
17 November 1944				293
26 November 1944				240
29 November 1944	H2		Southampton	313
3 December 1944				288
7 December 1944				
10 December 1944				
19 December 1944	H2		Stockbridge	318
29 December 1944	H2		Southampton	318
31 December 1944	H2		Chiseldon	320

A further 14 hospital trains arrived at Stourport between January and June 1945.

U.S Hospital Trains
Malvern Wells to Liverpool / Glasgow

Date	Train No.	Kidderminster Passing time		Destination
30 July 1944	H57	3.20 a.m	Loaded	LMS via Salop
	H57	3.50 p.m	Empty	Malvern Wells
18 August 1944	H57	7.43 a.m	Loaded	LMS via Salop
	H57	6.26 p.m	Empty	Malvern Wells
27 August 1944	H57	11.30 p.m	Empty	Malvern Wells
9 Sept 1944	H64	2.14 p.m	Empty	Malvern Wells
10 Sept 1944	H64	1.5 a.m	Loaded	LMS via Salop
	H57	1.38 a.m	Empty	Malvern Wells
12 Sept 1944	H57	8.25 a.m	Loaded	LMS via Salop
	H57	8.20 p.m	Empty	Malvern Wells
1 Oct 1944	H57	8.20 p.m	Empty	Malvern Wells
2 Oct 1944	H57	6.0 a.m	Loaded	LMS via Salop
	H57	5.25 p.m	Empty	Malvern Wells
3 Oct 1944	H57	7.45 a.m	Loaded	LMS via Salop
	H57	9.20 p.m	Empty	Malvern Wells
13 Oct 1944	H57	7.15 p.m	Empty	Malvern Wells
27 Oct 1944	H57	9.43 a.m	Loaded	LMS via Salop
	H57	9.13 p.m	Empty	Malvern Wells
28 Oct 1944	H57	5.35 p.m	Loaded	LMS via Salop
29 Oct 1944	H57	4.2 a.m	Empty	Malvern Wells
31 Oct 1944	H57	10.10 a.m	Loaded	LMS via Salop
	H57	9.13 p.m	Empty	Malvern Wells
21 Nov 1944	H57	1.15 a.m	Loaded	LMS via Salop
28 Nov 1944	H57	9.12 p.m	Empty	Malvern Wells
30 Nov 1944	H57	10.22 p.m	Empty	Malvern Wells
6 Dec 1944	H62	6.0 a.m	Loaded	LMS via Salop
21 Dec 1944	H57	10.40 p.m	Loaded	Glasgow via Salop
22 Dec 1944	H57	10.4 a.m	Empty	Malvern Wells
28 Dec 1944	H57	8.13 p.m	Empty	Malvern Wells

These hospital trains were transporting casualties from hospitals to ports for evacuation to the United States. The above list is an incomplete list of journeys during 1944.

The trains to and from Malvern Wells were usually in the hands of Worcester Castles, Stars or Halls. Locomotives noted include 4092 *Dunraven Castle,* 4051 *Saint Helena* and 6936 an un-named Hall.

U.S Hospital Trains
Newbury / Reading to LMS via Shrewsbury

Date	Train No.	Kidderminster Passing time	Destination		Locomotive
13 June 1944	H326	2.7 p.m	Reading	Empty	
1 July 1944	H326	11.33 p.m	Reading	Empty	
8 July 1944				Loaded	LNER 8518 + GW 6847
12 July 1944	H14		Ellesmere	Loaded	LNER 8525 + GW 6951
12 July 1944	H327	7.20 p.m	Reading	Empty	
28 July 1944	H59	1.40 p.m	Swindon	Empty	
6 August 1944	H326	5.15 p.m	Reading	Empty	
8 August 1944	H326	11.30 p.m	Reading	Empty	
16 September 1944	H64	12.50 p.m	Newbury	Empty	
6 October 1944	H327	1.57 a.m	Reading	Empty	
17 October 1944	H64	11.12 p.m	Newbury	Empty	
1 November 1944	H326	9.12 p.m	Reading	Empty	

British Hospital Trains
To Tettenhall and Wombourne

Date	Train No.		Locomotive
9 June 1944		to Tettenhall	5911 *Preston Hall* (NPT)
29 June 1944	H321	Shrivenham to Tettenhall	
5 July 1944	H66	Shrivenham to Tettenhall	
21 July 1944	H327	Shrivenham to Tettenhall	4999 *Gopsal Hall* (OXY)
30 July 1944	H66	Shrivenham to Tettenhall	4984 *Albrighton Hall* (SDN)
4 August 1944	H66	Shrivenham to Wombourne	4017 *Knight of Liege* (SDN)
8 August 1944	H56	Shrivenham to Wombourne	
10 August 1944	H56	Shrivenham to Wombourne	
13 August 1944	H66	Shrivenham to Wombourne	5900 *Hinderton Hall* (SDN)
14 August 1944	H56	Shrivenham to Wombourne	
19 August 1944	H66	Shrivenham to Wombourne	
24 August 1944	H56	Shrivenham to Wombourne	
29 August 1944	H66	Shrivenham to Wombourne	
9 September 1944	H66	Shrivenham to Wombourne	
17 September 1944	H66	Shrivenham to Wombourne	
20 September 1944	H56	Shrivenham to Wombourne	
25 September 1944	H66	Shrivenham to Wombourne	
30 September 1944	H56	Shrivenham to Wombourne	
15 October 1944	H66	Shrivenham to Wombourne	
30 October 1944	H56	Shrivenham to Wombourne	
3 November 1944	H56	Shrivenham to Wombourne	
9 November 1944	H56	Shrivenham to Wombourne	
29 November 1944	H66	Shrivenham to Wombourne	
15 December 1944	H66	Shrivenham to Wombourne	
14 January 1945	H66	Shrivenham to Wombourne	
9 February 1945	H56	Shrivenham to Wombourne	
25 February 1945	H56	Shrivenham to Wombourne	
6 March 1945	H56	Shrivenham to Wombourne	

30 March 1945	H66	Shrivenham to Wombourne	
13 April 1945	H56	Shrivenham to Wombourne	
23 April 1945	H65	Shrivenham to Wombourne	5911 *Preston Hall* (NPT)
8 May 1945	H56	Shrivenham to Wombourne	
24 May 1945	H66	Shrivenham to Wombourne	
9 June 1945	H66	Shrivenham to Wombourne	
30 June 1945	H65	Avonmouth to Wombourne	

Shrivenham was the entraining station for British casualties flown in to nearby airfields from the Continent.

The majority of the hospital trains from Shrivenham departed in the middle of the night, the passing times through Kidderminster were, therefore, usually during the hours of darkness and very few of the locomotives were recorded. After unloading at Tettenhall or Wombourne the trains proceeded to Oxley and returned to Shrivenham via Dudley and Kidderminster.

Troop Trains to stations in the Kidderminster area.

With the opening of U.S Army camps at Wolverley, Burlish Top (Camp Bewdley) and in the Wyre Forest area many special trains bringing troops from the docks at Liverpool and Glasgow arrived at local stations.

On 17 February 1943 two trains arrived at Kidderminster bringing the U.S 52nd. General Hospital who were to be based at Wolverley. These trains originated at Taunton where the unit had been staging. Arrival times at Kidderminster 12.40 pm and 1.40 pm.

On 21 December 1943 a train arrived at Bewdley from Glasgow bringing the U.S VIII Corps to Camp Bewdley

Two troop trains arrived at Stourport on 6 February 1944 as follows :
Train No. D3   Glasgow to Stourport   arrived 10.10 pm   load 11 Bogies + 2 Vans. 355 tons
        D4   Glasgow to Stourport   arrived 11.45 pm   load 12 Bogies + 2 Vans 380 tons
    Both these trains came via Shrewsbury and the Severn Valley Line. The empty stock working to Shrewsbury and the LMS via Bewdley, Kidderminster and Wolverhampton. GWR locomotives to and from Shrewsbury.

The Stourport portion of a troop train from Glasgow arrived on 21 February 1944.
Train No. D28   Glasgow to Stourport   arrived 12.20 am   load 3 bogies   90 tons
    This train was part of a train bound for South Wales which was split at Shrewsbury. The Stourport portion came via Wolverhampton and Hartlebury. GWR worked.

The arrival of the U.S 90th Infantry Division and its elements brought several troop trains to the district. Known details are as follows :

Date	Train No.		Arrival time	Load
4 April 1944	L1	Liverpool to Bridgnorth	7.58 pm	10 Bogies + 2 Vans 330 tons
	L4	Liverpool to Arley	11.18 pm	10 Bogies + 2 Vans 330 tons
5 April 1944	L8	Liverpool to Arley	12.18 am	10 Bogies + 2 Vans 330 tons
	L10	Liverpool to Bridgnorth	1.3 am	10 Bogies + 2 Vans 330 tons

93

Date	Train No.		Arrival time	Load		
5 April 1944	L15	Liverpool to Bridgnorth	7.17 a.m	10 Bogies + 2 Vans	330 tons	
	L19	Liverpool to Arley	11.26 a.m	10 Bogies + 2 Vans	330 tons	
	L21	Liverpool to Bridgnorth	12.1 p.m	10 Bogies + 2 Vans	330 tons	
	D51	Glasgow to Bridgnorth	8.35 p.m	9 Bogies + 2 Vans	305 tons	
6 April 1944	L47	Liverpool to Bridgnorth	5.50 a.m	10 Bogies + 2 Vans	330 tons	
9 April 1944	L36	Liverpool to Bridgnorth	10.47 p.m	9 Bogies + 1 Van	305 tons	
	L37	Liverpool to Bridgnorth	11.47 p.m	9 Bogies + 1 Van	305 tons	
	L34	Liverpool to Bewdley	9.34 p.m	11 Bogies + 2 Vans		
	L39	Liverpool to Bewdley	1.6 a.m	11 Bogies + 2 Vans	350 tons	
10 April 1944	L43	Liverpool to Bridgnorth	7.17 a.m	9 Bogies + 1 Van		
	L45	Liverpool to Arley	11.26 a.m	6 Bogies + 1 Van	190 tons	
	L44	Liverpool to Bewdley	8.37 a.m	11 Bogies + 2 Vans	350 tons	

All these trains came via Shrewsbury and the Severn Valley Line. The empty stock of trains L4, L8, L19, L34, L39, L44, and L45 returned to the LMS via Kidderminster and Oxley North.

Other trains arriving during April and May 1944 conveying U.S troops included :

Date	Train No.		Arrival time	Load		
17 April 1944		Glasgow to Kidderminster	1.45 p.m			
18 April 1944		Glasgow to Stourport	6.30 a.m			
19 April 1944	D97	Glasgow to Stourport	8.54 a.m	11 Bogies + 2 Vans	360 tons	
27 April 1944	D30	Glasgow to Bewdley	9.13 p.m	12 Bogies + 2 Vans		
28 April 1944	D1	Glasgow to Bewdley	8.33 p.m	12 Bogies + 2 Vans		
1 May 1944	L16	Liverpool to Stourport	5.40 p.m	10 Bogies + 2 Vans	320 tons	
3 May 1944	3W2	to Bewdley	2.52 p.m	8 Bogies	240 tons	
16 May `1944		Avonmouth to Stourport				
26 May 1944	D28	Glasgow to Bridgnorth	8.57 a.m	11 Bogies + 2 Vans	360 tons	
28 May 1944	D5	Glasgow to Hagley	9.55 p.m	11 Bogies + 2 Vans		

The empty stock of these trains returned to the LMS via Kidderminster and Oxley North except train D28 which returned to Shrewsbury via the Severn Valley Line.

After D-Day further trains arrived conveying U.S General Hospital Units for Camp Bewdley and Engineering Battalions for Sturt Common.

Date	Train No.		Arrival time	Load		
19 June 1944		Llandudno to Bewdley				
4 July 1944	D119	Glasgow to Bewdley	9.15 p.m	11 Bogies + 2 Vans	360 tons	
6 July 1944	L26	Liverpool to Bewdley	5.15 p.m	11 Bogies + 2 Vans	360 tons	
		Liverpool to Bewdley *				
13 July 1944	L4	Liverpool to Bridgnorth	6.40 p.m	11 Bogies + 2 Vans	360 tons	
6 August 1944		Glasgow to Bewdley **	8.0 p.m			
		Glasgow to Bewdley	12.0 m.n			

* Locomotive   LMS 2812 (22B)
** Locomotive   LMS 5308 (3A)

It was unusual for LMS locomotives to work through. The route taken by the through workings was probably via Crewe, Walsall and Dudley.

B= Bogie coaches   V= Vans for luggage

Troop Trains passing through Kidderminster in 1944

Date	Time	Train No.	Origin	Destination	Load
5 January	11.3 p.m	D.13	Glasgow	Basingstoke	11 B + 1 V
9 January	2.15 a.m	D.89	Glasgow	Culham	12 B + 1 V
10 January	10.50 a.m	D.53	Glasgow	Lambourn	11 B + 1 V
10 February	3.35 p.m	D.52	Glasgow	Cheltenham	9 B + 2 V
23 February	9.22 p.m	D.63	Glasgow	Broadway	13 B + 2 V
25 February	6.15 a.m	L.74	Liverpool	S.R via Reading	11 B + 1V
	11.49 p.m	D.45	Glasgow	Shipton	11 B + 2 V
6 March	12.44 p.m	6W3	Parkgate	S.R via Reading	6 B
20 March	2.38 p.m	20W1	Transfynydd	Kensington	8 B
29 March	11.40 a.m	29W9	Parkgate	S.R via Reading	6 B + 5 V
13 April	5.56 a.m	12SC6	Scotland	S.R via Reading	6 B + 5 V
	11.56 p.m	13W1	Ellesmere Port	Slough	10 B + 5 V
14 April	11.44 p.m	14W2	Crewe	Slough	9 B + 8 V
19 April	2.4 p.m	19W92	LMS via Salop	Winchcombe	13 B
22 April	2.38 p.m	22W1	Transfynydd	S.R via Acton	5 B + 1 V
29 April	11.9 a.m	29W5	Baschurch	Reading & S.R	9 B + 2 V
7 May	12.50 a.m	D.10	Glasgow	Reading & S.R	11 B + 2 V
	2.15 a.m	7W21	Wellington	Reading & S.R	10 B
12 May	3.6 p.m	12W2	LMS via Salop	Moreton in Marsh	9 B + 2 V
13 May	3.50 a.m	13W23	Wellington	Reading & S.R	11 B + 1 V
15 May	3.6 p.m	15W2	LMS via Salop	Moreton in Marsh	12 B + 2 V
19 May	12.55 p.m	19SC2	Scotland	Fladbury	9 B + 3 V
20 May	3.6 p.m	20W2	LMS via Salop	Moreton in Marsh	12 B + 3 V
27 May	12.36 p.m	27W4	LMS via Salop	Newbury	10 B + 1 V
17 June	5.36 a.m	17W27	Wrexham	Codford	10 B + 2 V
24 June	1.2 a.m	23W3	Overton on Dee	Sutton Scotney	11 B + 1 V
	8.19 a.m	24W1	Overton on Dee	Sutton Scotney	11 B + 1 V
7 July	1.48 p.m	7W1	LMS via Salop	Sutton Scotney	7 B + 1 V
8 July	3.8 p.m	8W3	LMS via Salop	Sutton Scotney	8 B + 1 V
	4.28 p.m	8W5	LMS via Salop	Sutton Scotney	8 B + 1 V
12 July	1.46 p.m	12W5	LMS via Salop	Sutton Scotney	11 B + 1 V
	3.4 p.m	12W7	LMS via Salop	Sutton Scotney	6 B + 1 V
13 July	12.53 p.m	13W10	LMS via Salop	Sutton Scotney	10 B + 1 V
14 July	4.17 p.m	14W3	Ledsham	Sutton Scotney	11 B + 1 V
15 July	4.17 p.m	15W3	Ledsham	Sutton Scotney	11 B + 1 V
20 July	3.4 p.m	20W5	Bettisfield	Sutton Scotney	8 B
	4.29 p.m	20W7	Bettisfield	Sutton Scotney	8 B + 1 V
	5.56 p.m	20W3	Adderley	Sutton Scotney	10 B + 1 V
22 July	1.48 p.m	22W1	Adderley	Sutton Scotney	6 B + 1 V
25 July	5.56 p.m	25W1	Ledsham	Sutton Scotney	7 B + 1 V
	7.44 p.m	25W14	LMS via Salop	Sutton Scotney	
26 July	5.56 p.m	26W12	LMS via Salop	Sutton Scotney	14 B +2 V
27 July	4.29 p.m	27W1	LMS via Salop	Sutton Scotney	
6 August	10.55 a.m	5SC30	Scotland	Taplow	12 B + 1 V
23 August	12.50 p.m	L24	Liverpool	Winchester	11 B + 2 V
24 August	5.52 p.m	L47	Liverpool	Winchester	11 B + 2 V
25 August	10.50 a.m	L57	Liverpool	Winchester	11 B + 2 V
8 November	12.49 p.m	8W6	Prestatyn	Beaconsfield	7 B + 1 V
19 November	5.1 p.m	18SC6	Scotland	Thame	
3 December	2.44 p.m	3N51	LNER	Winchcombe	10 B
5 December	2.3 p.m	5NA76	LMS	Worthy Down	
12 December	9.36 a.m	12F6	Cosford	Pontypool Road	

Government Stores Trains
E headlamps

During 1944 a large number of goods train carrying U.S Army supplies passed through Kidderminster. Passing times at Kidderminster not recorded. The destination of the majority of these trains was Birkenhead. The destination of the POL trains (petrol, oil & lubricants) from Stanlow and Port Sunlight was either Poole or Southampton.

These trains were all routed via Wombourne.

Date	Train No.			Load
8 January	8EL2BH	8.0 a.m	Long Marston to Birkenhead LNER via Wrexham	45
11 January	11DT1LP	2.0 a.m	Taplow to Liverpool LMS via Chester	40
		8.0 p.m	Harlescott to Taplow	50
12 January	12DC1BH	2.0 a.m	Didcot to Birkenhead	42
		8.0 p.m	Harlescott to SR via Reading	45
		6.0 p.m	Wem to Newbury	45
14 January		6.0 p.m	Wem to Newbury	45
15 January		8.0 p.m	Hartlebury to LMS via Chester	40
		8.0 p.m	Ellesmere to Avonmouth	50
16 January		6.0 p.m	Wem to Newbury	45
	16DC2BH	8.0 a.m	Didcot to Birkenhead	40
		8.0 a.m	Swindon to Birkenhead	35
17 January	17DC2BH	8.0 a.m	Didcot to Birkenhead	40
18 January	18DC2BH	8.0 a.m	Didcot to Birkenhead	40
		8.0 p.m	Hartlebury to LMS via Chester	45
		6.0 p.m	Wem to Newbury	45
22 January		8.0 p.m	Hartlebury to LMS via Chester	45
30 January		8.0 p.m	Didcot to Birkenhead	54
31 January		8.0 p.m	Stanlow to Wrangaton via Hooton	40
1 February		8.0 p.m	Hartlebury to CLC via Chester	45
		2.0 a.m	Didcot to Birkenhead	40
7 February		8.0 p.m	Stanlow to Wrangaton via Hooton	40
9 February	9AC4BH	8.0 p.m	Corsham to Birkenhead	41
10 February	10AC4BH	8.0 p.m	Corsham to Birkenhead	41
16 February	16DC1LP	2.0 a.m	Didcot to Liverpool LMS via Chester	45
17 February		2.0 a.m	Stanlow to Eastleigh	45
20 February		2.0 a.m	Stanlow to Eastleigh	45
	20EL3BH	2.0 p.m	Long Marston to Birkenhead via Saltney	41
22 February		2.0 a.m	Stanlow to Eastleigh	45
1 March	1AC1BH	2.0 a.m	Corsham to Birkenhead LNER via Wrexham	40
	1AC2LP	8.0 a.m	Corsham to Liverpool LMS via Chester	35
3 March		8.0 p.m	Corsham to Hookagate	40
12 March	12AC4BH	8.0 p.m	Corsham to Birkenhead LNER via Wrexham	41
14 March		2.0 a.m	Stanlow to Eastleigh	40
	14DC2BH	8.0 a.m	Didcot to Birkenhead LNER via Wrexham	45
	14DC4BH	8.0 p.m	Didcot to Birkenhead LNER via Wrexham	45
	14AC2LP	8.0 a.m	Corsham to Liverpool LMS via Chester	31
16 March		4.0 a.m	Stanlow to SR via Basingstoke	40
17 March		4.0 a.m	Stanlow to SR via Basingstoke	40
19 March		4.0 a.m	Stanlow to SR via Basingstoke	40
20 March		4.0 a.m	Stanlow to SR via Basingstoke	40
21 March		4.0 a.m	Stanlow to SR via Basingstoke	40
	21AC1BH	2.0 a.m	Corsham to Birkenhead LNER via Wrexham	38
22 March		4.0 a.m	Stanlow to SR via Basingstoke	40

	22EL2BH	8.0 a.m	Long Marston to Birkenhead LNER via Wrexham	34
23 March		4.0 a.m	Stanlow to SR via Basingstoke	40
		8.0 a,m	Stanlow to Wylye	40
24 March		4.0 a.m	Stanlow to SR via Basingstoke	40
26 March		8.0 a.m	Stanlow to Wylye	40
28 March		8.0 a.m	Stanlow to Wylye	40
30 March		8.0 a.m	Stanlow to Wylye	40
31 March		11.0 a.m	Stanlow to Brimscombe	40
1 April		8.0 p.m	Ince & Elton to Avonmouth	45
3 April		11.0 a.m	Stanlow to Brimscombe	40
5 April		11.0 a.m	Stanlow to Brimscombe	40
		8.0 p.m	Ince & Elton to Avonmouth	45
7 April		11.0 a.m	Stanlow to Brimscombe	40
8 April		9.0 a.m	Crewe to Wylye	40
10 April		11.0 a.m	Stanlow to Brimscombe	40
		9.0 a.m	Crewe to Wylye	40
12 April		9.0 a.m	Crewe to Wylye	40
		11.0 a.m	Stanlow to Brimscombe	40
16 April	16AC4BH	8.0 p.m	Corsham to Birkenhead via Hooton	30
	16DC1BH	2.0 a.m	Didcot to Birkenhead via Hooton	45
		6.0 a.m	Stanlow to Wylye	40
17 April		8.0 p.m	Ince & Elton to Brimscombe	40
19 April		9.30 a.m	Crewe to Wylye	40
		8.0 p.m	Ince & Elton to Brimscombe	40
20 April		8.0 p.m	Ince & Elton to Andover	45
21 April		9.30 a.m	Crewe to Wylye	40
		8.0 p.m	Ince & Elton to Andover	45
22 April		8.0 p.m	Ince & Elton to Brimscombe	45
23 April		9.30 a.m	Crewe to Wylye	40
25 April		9.30 a.m	Crewe to Wylye	40
27 April		9.30 a.m	Crewe to Wylye	40
29 April		9.30 a.m	Crewe to Wylye	40
30 April	30DC3BH	2.0 p.m	Didcot to Birkenhead LNER via Wrexham	40
	30EL3BH	2.0 p.m	Long Marston to Birkenhead via Hooton	31
9 May		8.0 p.m	Ince & Elton to Wylye	45
		9.30 p.m	Chester to Long Marston	35
12 May		8.0 p.m	Ince & Elton to Wylye	45
14 May		8.0 p.m	Ince & Elton to Basingstoke	45
16 May		8.0 p.m	Ince & Elton to Basingstoke	45
31 May		12.30 a.m	Basingstoke to Birkenhead LNER via Wrexham	30
	31KY2BH	8.0 a.m	Westbury to Birkenhead LNER via Wrexham	50
	31KY1BH	8.0 p.m	Westbury to Birkenhead LNER via Wrexham	50
	31KT3BH	2.0 p.m	Newbury/Thatcham to Birkenhead LNER via Wrexham	50
1 June	1KN4BH	8.0 p.m	Honeybourne to Birkenhead LNER via Wrexham	50
	1KT3BH	2.0 p.m	Newbury/Thatcham to Birkenhead LNER via Wrexham	50
	1KT4BH	8.0 p.m	Newbury/Thatcham to Birkenhead LNER via Wrexham	50
2 June	2KN3BH	2.0 p.m	Honeybourne to Birkenhead LNER via Wrexham	50
	2KN4BH	8.0 p.m	Honeybourne to Birkenhead LNER via Wrexham	50
	2DC3BH	2.0 p.m	Didcot to Birkenhead GWR via Hooton	42
	2MG1BH	2.0 a.m	Highbridge to Birkenhead LNER via Wrexham	44
		2.0 a.m	Laira to Birkenhead LNER via Wrexham	50
3 June	3DC3BH	2.0 p.m	Didcot to Birkenhead LNER via Wrexham	50
	3KN3BH	2.0 p.m	Honeybourne to Birkenhead LNER via Wrexham	50

Government Stores Trains (contd)

Date	Code	Time	Route	No.
6 June	6KN2BH	8.0 a.m	Honeybourne to Birkenhead LNER via Wrexham	50
	6KN4BH	8.0 p.m	Honeybourne to Birkenhead LNER via Wrexham	50
	6KT2BH	1.0 p.m	Newbury/Thatcham to Birkenhead GWR via Hooton	50
	6KT3BH	2.0 p.m	Newbury/Thatcham to Birkenhead LNER via Wrexham	42
	6KT4BH	8.0 p.m	Newbury/Thatcham to Birkenhead LNER via Wrexham	40
	6KY4BH	8.0 p.m	Westbury to Birkenhead LNER via Wrexham	50
		3.0 p.m	Laira to Birkenhead LNER via Wrexham	36
7 June	7KN1BH	2.0 a.m	Honeybourne to Birkenhead LNER via Wrexham	50
	7KN3BH	2.0 a.m	Honeybourne to Birkenhead LNER via Wrexham	50
	7KT1BH	2.0 a.m	Newbury/Thatcham to Birkenhead LNER via Wrexham	40
	7KN4BH	8.0 p.m	Honeybourne to Birkenhead LNER via Wrexham	50
	7KY4BH	8.0 p.m	Westbury to Birkenhead LNER via Wrexham	44
	7KY3BH	2.0 p.m	Westbury to Birkenhead LNER via Wrexham	50
		3.0 a.m	Laira to Birkenhead LNER via Wrexham	50
	MO1PLH	2.0 a.m	Stanlow to Poole Harbour via Winchester	48
8 June	8KN3BH	2.0 p.m	Honeybourne to Birkenhead LNER via Wrexham	50
	8KY3BH	2.0 p.m	Westbury to Birkenhead LNER via Wrexham	40
		8.0 p.m	Westbury to Birkenhead LNER via Wrexham	43
9 June	9MG1BH	2.0 a.m	Highbridge to Birkenhead LNER via Wrexham	50
	9AC4BH	8.0 p.m	Corsham to Birkenhead	40
		2.0 p.m	Westbury to Birkenhead LNER via Wrexham	40
		3.30 p.m	LMS via Shrewsbury to Winchester	35
		2.0 a.m	Newbury to Birkenhead LNER via Wrexham	42
		8.0 a.m	Corsham to Birkenhead	44
10 June		8.0 a.m	Corsham to Birkenhead	40
		5.0 a.m	Chester to SR via Winchester	45
	10RS2SA	2.0 p.m	Stanlow to Southampton via Winchester	28
	10MO1PLH	2.0 a.m	Stanlow to Poole Harbour via Winchester	44
11 June		2.0 a.m	Didcot to Birkenhead LNER via Wrexham	50
		8.0 a.m	Corsham to Birkenhead LNER via Wrexham	40
12 June		8.0 p.m	Stanlow to SR via Winchester	33
		2.0 a.m	Didcot to Birkenhead	45
		8.0 a.m	Corsham to Birkenhead LNER via Wrexham	40
13 June		2.0 a.m	Longmoor to Birkenhead	50
21 June		8.0 a.m	Corsham to Birkenhead	40
23 June		8.0 a.m	Stanlow to SR via Winchester	36
24 June		2.0 a.m	Stanlow to SR via Winchester	36
		8.0 a.m	Stanlow to SR via Winchester	36
25 June		8.0 a.m	Corsham to Birkenhead via Hooton	40
		8.0 a.m	Port Sunlight to SR via Winchester	40
16 July		5.0 a.m	Corsham to Birkenhead LNER via Wrexham	40
		12.30 a.m	Andover to Birkenhead	40
		6.30 a.m	Andover to Birkenhead LNER via Wrexham	40
		8.0 a.m	Swindon to Birkenhead	40
		5.0 a.m	Steventon to Birkenhead	40
		11.0 p.m	Steventon to Birkenhead	40
17 July		2.0 a.m	Steventon to Birkenhead	40
		8.0 a.m	Swindon to Birkenhead	40
		11.0 p.m	Didcot to Birkenhead	34
22 July		8.0 a.m	Long Marston to Birkenhead LNER via Wrexham	40
		8.0 p.m	Didcot to Birkenhead LNER via Wrexham	50
23 July		2.0 a.m	Didcot to Birkenhead LNER via Wrexham	44
		2.0 a.m	Donnington to SR via Winchester	50

"FOREIGN" Locomotives
Seen at Kidderminster in Wartime

U.S.A S160 2-8-0 Locomotives

The first U.S.A locomotive to be noted at Kidderminster was 1611 (OXY) on an up goods on 14 February 1943. This was to be the first of many to be seen over the next 18 months. Very often two or three would be seen in a day on goods trains.

They were painted in a light grey livery with white lettering. Some were branded U.S.A and others TRANSPORTATION CORPS U.S.A.

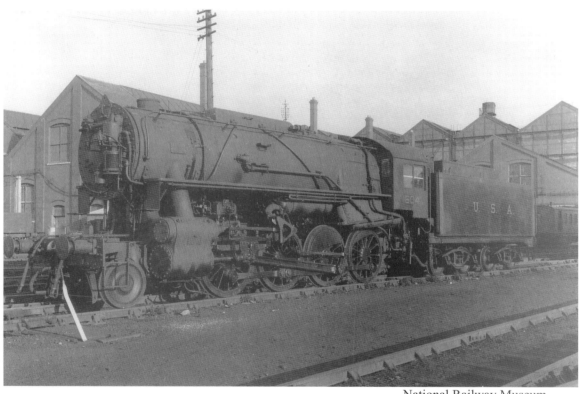

National Railway Museum

1604 outside Swindon Works

U.S.A 2-8-0s noted at Kidderminster on Goods Trains were :

1601 (NPT) 10 March 1943	1602 (PPRD) 13 April 1943	1603 (PPRD) 19 February 1943
1604 (NPT) 10 April 1943	1605 (STB) 16 March 1943	1606 (SDN) 7 June 1943
1607 (CDF) 6 March 1943	1608 (OXY) 17 March 1943	1609 (CDF) 12 March 1943
1610 (CNYD) 15 August 1943	1611 (STB) 14 February 1943	1612 (OXY) 7 April 1943
1613 (OXY) 5 March 1943	1614 (OXY) 9 April 1943	1615 (SALOP) 20 August 1944
1616 (PPRD) 31 March 1943	1618 (OXY) 7 March 1943	1619 (NPT) 2 April 1943
1620 (OXY) 13 February 1944	1621 (STB) 24 February 1943	1622 (OXY) 7 April 1943

1623 (PPRD)	6 March 1943	1624 (NPT)	17 March 1943	1632 (SPM)	19 July 1944
1639 (STJ)	12 Sept 1943	1642 (LLY)	5 January 1944	1643 (GLO)	17 May 1944
1644 (GLO)	28 March 1944	1645 (GLO)	12 June 1944	1646 (CHR)	31 October 1943
1647 (OXY)	7 September 1943	1649 (OXY)	5 January 1944	1651 (NPT)	8 January 1944
1654 (BAN)	31 October 1943	1655 (CDF)	3 January 1944	1658 (BAN)	17 October 1943
1661 (HFD)	7 July 1944	1662 (PDN)	9 June 1944	1663 (OXF)	18 July 1944
1664 (LLY)	21 May 1944	1681 (SPM)	10 May 1944	1682 (SPM)	28 Dec 1943
1683 (SPM)	28 March 1944	1684 (WOS)	13 April 1944	1687 (SPM)	7 January 1944
1689 (DID)	19 October 1943	1749 (SPM)	18 August 1944	1757 (SPM)	7 June 1944
1835 (PPRD)	24 March 1943	1841 (OXY)	27 July 1943	1877 (PDN)	30 July 1944
1881 (ABDR)	7 July 1943	1883 (NPT)	14 August 1943	1891 (OXF)	26 August 1943
1892 (NPT)	14 August 1944	1893 (STJ)	30 June 1944	1894 (PPRD)	18 July 1943
1895 (NPT)	26 June 1943	1896 (CDF)	28 Dec 1943	1899 (ABDR)	27 April 1944
1900 (SALOP)	24 July 1944	1901 (SALOP)	10 Sept 1943	1902 (OXY)	21 July 1943
1909 (CDF)	10 Nov 1943	1910 (OXY)	26 Sept 1943	1913 (SPM)	3 Sept 1943
1914 (SDN)	30 March 1944	1915 (DID)	28 Nov 1943	2096 (PDN)	14 July 1943
2098 (OXF)	12 October 1943	2100 (PDN)	8 July 1943	2110 (OXY)	6 July 1943
2112 (PPRD)	23 Nov 1943	2120 *	10 October 1944	2122 (SPM)	14 Sept 1943
2129 (PDN)	22 August 1943	2130 (SDN)	14 May 1944	2131 (PDN)	25 July 1944
2132 (BAN)	29 July 1943	2133 (OXY)	8 October 1943	2134 (BAN)	4 Sept 1943
2135 (OXY)	30 July 1943	2136 (OXY)	9 October 1943	2137 (TYS)	9 Oct 1943
2138 (OXY)	1 January 1944	2139 (NPT)	10 August 1943	2140 (OXY)	1 Nov 1943
2141 (SDN)	7 November 1943	2144 (CDF)	11 Sept 1943	2145 (PDN)	3 August 1943
2147 (BAN)	29 August 1943	2148 (PDN)	9 March 1944	2149 (CDF)	12 August 1943
2150 (PPRD)	29 July 1943	2151 (PDN)	9 August 1943	2154 **	9 May 1944
2164 (SPM)	13 May 1944	2267 (LDR)	7 Nov 1943	2270 (GLO)	6 March 1944
2279 (HFD)	13 April 1944	2280 (PDN)	27 May 1944	2290 (LLY)	1 August 1944
2294 (CDF)	7 May 1944	2312 (NPT)	4 June 1944	2313 (STJ)	20 July 1943
2315 (NEA)	4 November 1943	2318 (PDN)	28 July 1943	2319 (NPT)	4 Sept 1943
2323 (NPT)	31 July 1943	2324 (NPT)	2 October 1943	2326 (TYS)	17 Oct 1943
2338 (WOS)	13 April 1944	2339 (NEA)	2 April 1944	2349 (NEA)	26 Sept 1943
2351 (NEA)	3 October 1943	2353 (GLO)	8 April 1944	2354 (TYS)	7 August 1943
2357 (WOS)	4 January 1944	2358 (NEA)	30 December 1943	2360 (OXY)	18 Sept 1943
2363 ***	16 September 1943	2368 (STJ)	6 September 1943	2369 (STJ)	8 July 1944
2403 (NPT)	19 August 1943	2404 (SDN)	12 January 1944	2405 (STJ)	13 Oct 1943
2407 (NPT)	29 September 1943	2408 (SPM)	11 March 1944	2410 (NEA)	27 July 1944
2414 ****	15 September 1943	2417 ****	3 August 1943	2430 (DID)	17 Feb 1944
2432 (SPM)	3 May 1944	2434 (WES)	24 Nov 1943	2435 (HFD)	11 Jan 1944
2439 (TYS)	3 September 1943	2440 (BAN)	23 April 1944	2441 (BAN)	16 April 1944
2443 (HFD)	10 April 1944	2448 (TYS)	6 May 1944	2450 (SPM)	6 November 1943
2640 *****	12 October 1944				

*   en route to Southampton for shipment to continent ex LNER

**   on test run from Newport ex Treforest store.

***   en route to LNER from Cardiff Docks?

****   en route to Mold Junction (LMS) from Cardiff Docks?

*****   light engine from Liverpool to Southampton for shipment to continent

U.S.A 0-6-0T

For shunting purposes in Army Depots and Port Areas a small 0-6-0T locomotive was designed and built in the United States for the Transportation Corps.

They were occasionally to be seen passing through Kidderminster to or from Worcester works or transferring from one depot to another.

No.1942   25 February 1944   Worcester Works to Melbourne Military Railway.

No.1407   14 June 1944   En route to the U.S Depot at Newport Ebbw prior to Shipment to the Continent.

Derek Plumb

U.S.A 0-6-0T No. 1390 in store at Newbury Race Course
shortly after the end of the war.

U.S.A 0-4-0 Petrol

7770, 7771 and 7772 were noted in an up goods en route to Southampton on 12 June 1944.

LMS (WD) 2-8-0 Class 8F

At the beginning of the war the WD adapted as standard for locomotive construction the LMS Class 8F 2-8-0. These were intended for use on the Continent, but following the fall of France they were not needed for that purpose and 25 were loaned to the GWR.

Prior to operation on the GWR they passed through Wolverhampton Stafford Road works for modifications. Noted passing through Kidderminster light engine en route from Wolverhampton to their new depot at Newport were :

8288 + 8289 on 10 September 1940 and 8290 on 11 September 1940

Others noted on goods trains while on loan to the GWR were :

8226 (STJ)	30 April 1941	8286 (NPT)	19 February 1941
8237 (STJ)	21 June 1941	8287 (NEA)	15 April 1941
8240 (LLY)	13 November 1940	8291 (NPT)	14 September 1940
8242 (NPT)	23 November 1940	8293 (NPT)	2 March 1941
8243 (NEA)	19 December 1940	8294 (CDF)	15 February 1941
8244 (LLY)	15 November 1940	8295 (NPT)	9 August 1941
8253 (NPT)	24 December 1940	8296 (LDR)	19 December 1940
8257 (NPT)	10 June 1941	8300 (NPT)	10 March 1941
8261 (NPT)	9 April 1941		

They were all returned to the War Department by October 1941 except 8293 which was involved in an accident at Slough in July 1941. This locomotive was returned to the LMS in February 1942.

The original WD numbers allocated to these locomotives were as follows :

8226 - 8263 series WD 300 -337   built North British

8286 – 8300 series WD 400 -414   built Beyer Peacock

Les W Perkins

LMS 2-8-0 Class 8F No. 8444

A further 80 LMS Class 8F 2-8-0s numbered 8400 - 8479 were constructed at Swindon between 1943 and 1945. They carried their number on the buffer beam in the GWR style, and with the power classification E on the cab side. They were loaned to the GWR and were allocated to sheds ranging from Birkenhead to Penzance. 8400 (SPM) was the first to be noted at Kidderminster on 5 August 1943. Subsequently every member of the class came through Kidderminster on goods trains before they were transferred to the LMS in 1946/47. None were ever observed on passenger trains.

LNER 2-8-0 Class 04

In November 1940 the LNER loaned 30 Class 04 2-8-0s to the GWR. These locomotives were identical to the 30XX RODs in Great Western ownership. They soon became a familiar sight on goods trains passing through Kidderminster.

Those noted were :

5393 (CHR)	23 February 1941	6205 (SHL)	4 December 1940
6220 (OXY)	27 August 1941	6231 (STB)	13 June 1941
6258 (NPT)	4 May 1941	6265 (NPT)	25 February 1941
6277 (OXY)	28 March 1942	6295 (SALOP)	13 August 1942
6321 (OXY)	23 December 1940	6350 (TYS)	9 April 1941
6365 (TYS)	9 April 1941	6524 (OXY)	9 May 1941
6540 (OXY)	17 April 1941	6562 (PDN)	31 May 1942
6566 (PDN)	18 July 1941	6586 (BAN)	16 March 1941
6594 (BL)	11 October 1942	6595 (SALOP)	31 May 1941
6621 (OXY)	18 April 1941	6633 (OXY)	7 April 1941
6639 ((OXY)	7 December 1940		

All these were returned to the LNER by February 1943.

A. Norman H. Glover

GWR No. 3043 at Tyseley in 1949.

WD British Austerity 2-8-0

To replace the U.S.A 2-8-0s a number of British Austerity 2-8-0s were loaned to the GWR in September 1944. The following were noted on goods trains passing through Kidderminster :

7011 (OXY)	4 October 1944		7043 (WOS)	29 September 1944
7044 (OXY)	21 September 1944		7047 (OXY)	30 October 1944
7048 (OXY)	20 September 1944		7087 (NPT)	22 September 1944
7140 (STB)	28 September 1944		7141 (STB)	26 November 1944
7144 (TYS)	12 November 1944		7146 (SALOP)	27 September 1944
7150 (OXY)	23 September 1944		7233 (WOS)	5 October 1944
7234 (OXY)	5 October 1944		7244 (BAN)	2 November 1944
7259 (NEA)	26 September 1944		7262 (BAN)	28 October 1944
7385 (SPM)	28 October 1944		7399 (SPM)	28 September 1944
7400 (WOS)	26 September 1944		7414 (NPT)	16 October 1944
7415 (NPT)	4 October 1944		7416 (SALOP)	9 October 1944
7419 (STB)	23 September 1944		7451 (PPRD)	18 October 1944
7454 (NEA)	4 October 1944		7457 (SDN)	7 October 1944
7458 (WOS)	30 October 1944		7461 (WOS)	13 October 1944
7465 (PDN)	12 October 1944		7489 (RDG)	22 September 1944
7490 (DID)	14 October 1944		7491 (OXF)	21 September 1944
7493 (OXF)	21 October 1944		7495 (RDG)	25 September 1944
7497 (OXF)	7 October 1944			

These were all returned to the WD by March 1945 and shipped to the Continent.

A further 89 were loaned to the GWR in 1946 /47. They were classified E Blue by the GWR. By this time they had had 70,000 added to their numbers. After the railways were nationalised in 1948 they were renumbered by British Railways in the 9XXXX series.

They were extremely common on goods trains and all had been observed at Kidderminster by the end of 1949.

After serving on the continent large numbers were stored, pending overhaul, at various locations in this country. Several were noted being hauled dead through Kidderminster from the dump at Kingham en route to works.

    8 February 1947   77004 + 79229

    11 February 1947   77006 + 78564 + 77315 hauled by 6347 (NEY)

These were subsequently allocated to the LNER.

LNER 4-6-0 Class B7

An unusual stranger noted passing through Kidderminster on 7 January 1942 on an up goods train was LNER 4-6-0 Class B7 No. 5459 which was shedded at Woodford Halse (near Banbury).

It may have been working a Banbury turn back to its home shed.

Rex Conway collection

LNER Class B7 No. 5459

L.N.E.R 0-6-0 Class J.25
'Spitfires'

Following the requisition by the War Department of a number of Dean 0-6-0s the GWR received 40 old North Eastern Railway 0-6-0s Class J.25 designed by William Worsdell and built from 1898 to 1902. Several of these had already been withdrawn by the LNER and hastily reconditioned.

The first J.25s to be noted at Kidderminster were 2076 on 16 December 1939 and 2071 and 2135 coupled together on 18 December 1939. These were en route from Wolverhampton to Gloucester.

Locally, Worcester had the largest allocation of these, 10 being initially allocated in January and February 1940. These were 1986, 2040, 2051, 2058, 2061, 2065, 2075, 2138, 2141 and 2142.

Shrewsbury had three – 257, 536 and 2059 which were used on goods trains on the Severn Valley line to Hartlebury and Kidderminster. The Worcester and Shrewsbury J.25s monopolised the goods workings on the Severn Valley line. Local goods between Worcester and Kidderminster were often with J.25s from Worcester shed.

Other local sheds to receive J.25s were Stourbridge and Hereford, 29, 1973, 2000 and 2126 at Stourbridge and 1994, 2053 and 2072 at Hereford.

The Hereford ones could be seen on the Hereford, Tenbury, Stourbridge Junc goods on which the Stourbridge ones worked on alternate days. The Elmley Lovett goods for the R.A.F 25MU depot was often in the hands of J.25s from Stourbridge.

Kidderminster shed received its first J.25 in October 1941 when 2040 was transferred from Worcester. It was mainly used on goods between Alveley, Stourport and Hartlebury. This loco was frequently exchanged for other Worcester J.25s over the next couple of years.

Local railwaymen referred to the J.25s as 'Spitfires', whether this was due to their burst of speed is doubtful!

In 1943 some of the above mentioned locomotives were returned to the LNER, they were 1973 and 2000 from Stourbridge, 2058, 2065 and 2141 from Worcester.

By 1944 Worcester had transferred most of their remaining J.25s to Kidderminster, when six or more could be seen on shed on a Sunday including 1986, 1989, 1994, 2040, 2051, 2053, 2071, 2134 and 2142.

The electric motors in the pumping house at Butts Siding, Worcester were away for repair at the end of September 1944 and two J.25s 1989 and 2040 from Kidderminster to provide steam for the emergency steam engines. The pumps drew water from the Severn to the yards at Shrub Hill.

In December 1945 the reign of the J.25s was drawing to a close. Kidderminster dispatched the following to Darlington, some via Wrexham and others via Banbury.

18 December 1945   1994
31 December 1945   5704 (renumbered from 2051) and 2053
 1 January 1946   1986 and 2040
 2 January 1946   1989

The final two were 5722 (renumbered from 2136) to Darlington 29 August 1946 and 5723 (renumbered from 2138) to Darlington 8 November 1946.

LMS 0-6-0 Class 2F

In addition to the 40 Class J25s received on loan from the LNER the GWR also received 40 LMS Class 2F 0-6-0s.ex Midland Railway of 1878 vintage. Initially these were allocated in the London and Bristol divisions and were rarely seen at Kidderminster. However a few were noted on goods trains.

21 June 1940	3038 (DID)	22 June 1940	3081 (SHL)
6 July 1940	3108 (DID)	15 October 1941	3027 (OXF)
12 August 1943	3372 (OXF)	11 July 1944	3048 (WES)
12 May 1945	3109 (OXF)		

3048 was probably on loan to either Kidderminster or Worcester during the summer of 1944 as it was noted several times on local goods workings.

3027 was on loan to Kidderminster from 24 January until 19 March 1942 for working the Highley coal trains.

3109 was noted proceeding to Kidderminster shed coupled to LNER J25 2071. An interesting combination!

All the LMS 0-6-0s were returned to their parent company by the end of 1945.

H.C.C Casserley

LMS Class 2F 0-6-0 No. 3109.

SR 4-4-2T Class I3

In 1942 two SR 4-4-2Ts 2089 and 2091 were allocated to Worcester. They were used on passenger trains between Worcester and Wolverhampton.

They were regularly to be seen on the following departures from Kidderminster :

7.10 am to Birmingham (as far as Stourbridge Junction)

11.28 am and 9.28 pm to Worcester SH

7.0 pm to Wolverhampton

2089 was in green livery and 2091 was in black livery.

Rex Conway collection

SR 4-4-2T Class I3 No. 2091

SR 4-6-0 'Remembrance' Class (N15X)

Locomotives of this class were occasionally to be seen at Kidderminster on goods trains. On 23 April 1943 2330 *Cudworth* (PDN) was seen on a southbound goods. It was also noted on a sugar beet train in the autumn of 1942.

They were returned to the Southern Railway in July 1943.

Rex Conway collection

SR 'Remembrance' (N15X) 4-6-0 No. 2330 *Cudworth*

PRIVATE AND NOT FOR PUBLICATION   NOTICE No. 830

GREAT WESTERN RAILWAY
(For use of the Company's Servants only.)

Birmingham Division

NOTICE SHOWING THE
ARRANGEMENTS

FOR THE

DIVERSION OF TRAINS

TO

ALTERNATIVE ROUTES

IN CASES OF

EMERGENCY

Receipt of this Notice to be acknowledged to
the Head of Department by FIRST Train.

F. R. POTTER,
Superintendent of the Line.

25th September, 1940.

Extracts from the above Special Notice

Route Obstructed.   **Code B.M.D. 6**
Between Tyseley (South) and Handsworth Junction.
ALTERNATIVE ROUTE.

Down trains may be diverted at Old Oak Common, Oxford, Honeybourne West, or at Hatton to run via West Midland Line to Wolverhampton or via Bicester Line, Leamington Spa, Stratford-on-Avon, Worcester, and West Midland Line.

Up trains may be diverted at Priestfield Junction to run via West Midland Line, Stratford-on-Avon, Leamington Spa, and Bicester or West Midland Line, Oxford and Old Oak Common, or West Midland Line and Honeybourne West.

Route Obstructed.   **Code W.D. 8**
Worcester and Hartlebury Junction.
ALTERNATIVE ROUTE.
Via Honeybourne, Stratford-on-Avon, and North Warwickshire Line.

Route Obstructed.   **Code W.D. 10**
Between Kidderminster Junction and Stourbridge Junction (North).
ALTERNATIVE ROUTE.
Via Honeybourne, Stratford-on-Avon, and North Warwick Line.

On 23 November 1940 some Paddington to Birmingham / Wolverhampton trains were diverted via Honeybourne, Worcester and Kidderminster in accordance with Code B.M.D.6 due to enemy action at Birmingham Snow Hill and Moor Street.

LMS Diversions via Kidderminster

As a result of enemy action in the Birmingham area during 1940 and 1941 LMS passenger trains between Bradford, Derby and Bristol were diverted via Water Orton, Walsall, Dudley, Kidderminster and Worcester on a number of occasions.

Following an air raid during the night of 15 October 1940, during which a number of bombs fell in the Curzon Street area adjacent to the Derby line, a number of goods trains hauled by Class 3F and 4F 0-6-0s were diverted.

Noted through Kidderminster were :

Friday 18 October 1940	4244 (18C)
Saturday 19 October 1940	4173 (17A)
Sunday 20 October 1940	3462 (22B), 4102 (22C), 4241 (18A), 4406 (21A), 4586 (16B)
Monday 21 October 1940	3433 (21A)

Thursday 14 November 1940, 5286 (19B) was noted on a Bradford to Bristol express.

On Saturday 23 November 1940 the Holliday Street tunnel at Birmingham New Street was blocked by falling masonry until around mid-day. Diverted passenger trains noted were :

910 (20A),   5231 (10C)
5557 *New Brunswick* (22A)
3978 (22B) on goods

The tunnels at Birmingham New Street were again blocked on 10/11 April 1941 resulting in further diversions. No less than 11 Jubilees were seen at Kidderminster over the two days.

Thursday 10 April 1940	5585 *Hyderabad* (19B)	5595 *Southern Rhodesia* (20A)	
	5618 *New Hebrides* (22A)	5639 *Raleigh* (14B)	
	5696 *Arethusa* (17A)	5724 *Warspite* (20A)	
	5726 *Vindictive* (20A)	5036 (20A)	
	5093 (20A)	5276 (20A)	
	Also 2-6-2T No.11 on a passenger train!		
Friday 11 April 1941	5566 *Queensland* (20A)	5656 *Cochrane* (17A)	
	5725 *Repulse* (20A)	5573 *Newfoundland* (19B)	
	5030 (10A)	5534 *E.Tootal Broadhurst* (20A) Patriot	
	3921 (16B) and 4155 (16B) were on goods trains.		

On Wednesday 30 April 1941 a goods train was derailed on the Lickey incline at Bromsgrove resulting in diversions via Kidderminster.

5568 *Western Australia* (20A)   5664 *Nelson* (19B)
5538 *Giggleswick* (20A) Patriot   5089 (20A)
5273 (21A)   326 (21A)
1002 (22B)   3948 (16A) goods

On Sunday 11 May 1941 the line was blocked at Stoke Works by bomb damage and an unexploded bomb.

4039 (16A) noted at Kidderminster on a goods train.

LMS SHED CODES

3C = Walsall   10A = Springs Branch   10C = Patricroft   14B = Kentish Town   16A = Nottingham
16B = Peterborough   17A = Derby   18A = Toton   18C = Hasland   19B = Millhouses
20A = Leeds   21A = Saltley   22A = Bristol   22B = Gloucester   22C = Bath

TWO HIGH EXPLOSIVE BOMBS DROPPED NEAR RAILWAY
SUNDAY 3rd NOVEMBER 1940

Lone Raider Drops from Clouds

Hundreds of people in a West Midland town had their first glimpse of a German 'plane on Sunday afternoon when a lone raider dropped from the clouds, flew over the town, and released two bombs which fell on either side of the road leading to a football ground.

One bomb exploded harmlessly in the grounds of a derelict house which has been unoccupied for some years and was falling into ruins—a process hastened by the blast from the bomb! Far more potentially dangerous was the bomb which dropped on tennis courts across the road. The courts formerly formed part of the grounds of a Vicarage, and the Vicarage itself has been, converted into two semi-detached houses. The occupants of the one nearest to the explosion, a man, his wife and their four-year-old son, all received superficial injuries. The dining room door was blown off its hinges, striking the man on the head. His wife and their little boy both received cuts from flying glass, but the injuries of all three were treated on the spot, as were those of a woman in the adjoining house.

Many windows were shattered in the nearby housing estate, doors were blown in and wooden erections wrecked, while tiles were hurled from the roof in several cases. Clods of earth and fragments of timber also strewed the road. Glass in the side of a grandstand on the nearby football field was broken.

Police and members of the A.R.P. services dealt promptly with the situation. The debris was cleared, the apertures which had been windows were covered by roofing felt, and steps were taken to make damaged houses watertight.

The raid occurred while the afternoon service was in progress at local churches. At one of them a Church of England dignitary had referred in his sermon to the debased philosophy of "Mein Kampf," when the noise of the explosions in another part of the town was clearly heard. He spoke reassuringly to the congregation, advising them that they could leave if they wished, but would be safer if they stayed where they were. Most of those present concurred, and the service proceeded. In other churches where the service was in progress the congregation stayed put.

Kidderminster Shuttle Friday 8th November 1940

RAILWAYMEN HOME GUARD

Inspection by Colonel K. W. C. Grand

Members of the G.W.R. platoon, Home Guard, "C" Company, 6th Battalion, Worcestershire Regiment, paraded in the Station Drive on Sunday for inspection They were under the command of Major W H. X. Smith (Company officer) and Lieut. J Ferguson, M.M. J.P.

The inspecting officer was Colonel K. W. C. Grand assistant general manager of the G.W.R. at Paddington, and liason officer to Home Guard units on the G.W.R. system. Others present were Mr J. F. M Taylor (Divisional Supt.), Mr T H Hollingsworth (District Goods Manager), Mr. R J Armstrong (Divisional Locomotive Superintendent), Mr G. E. R Penney (assistant divisional superintendent) all of Worcester, and Mr. R. G Randall, the Kidderminster Goods Agent

Colonel Grand saw the platoon at drill, inspected the men's equipment and took the salute. Addressing the parade he congratulated officers and men on their smart turn-out Evidently they realised the serious job to which they devoted most of their energies after working hours in war service He had noted a feeling in some quarters that in view of the Allies recent victories in North Africa and the Near East, we could now slacken the war effort That was a fallacy It behoved us to be even more alert and prepared for surprise attacks. Hitler was a gangster and in desperation at the turn of tide on the war fronts might attack us on the home front at any time. The Home Guard was doing excellent work and by becoming progressively proficient made it possible to release more of the regular Army for active service abroad. He was proud to see the patriotism of railway workers in sacrificing spare time to be of greater service in defence of their country

Kidderminster Shuttle Friday 3rd July 1943

Luftwaffe Reconnaissance photograph taken 1,42 p.m 8th November 1940
5 days after the raid. Arrows indicate bomb craters.

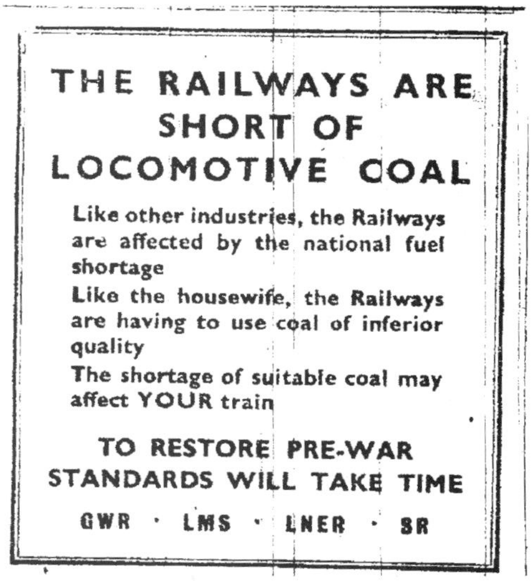

THE RAILWAYS ARE SHORT OF LOCOMOTIVE COAL

Like other industries, the Railways are affected by the national fuel shortage

Like the housewife, the Railways are having to use coal of inferior quality

The shortage of suitable coal may affect YOUR train

TO RESTORE PRE-WAR STANDARDS WILL TAKE TIME

GWR · LMS · LNER · SR

THE RAILWAYS ARE SHORT OF CARRIAGES

Every day 3,500 war-worn carriages — one eighth of the total stock — are out of action

Some are undergoing repair. Others must await attention because skilled labour and materials are not fully available

This daily shortage of 180,000 seats may affect YOUR train

TO RESTORE PRE-WAR STANDARDS WILL TAKE TIME

GWR · LMS · LNER · SR

THE RAILWAYS ARE SHORT OF TRAINED STAFF

Nearly 100,000 skilled railwaymen, one-sixth of the Railways' staffs, have still to be demobilised

When they return, their skill and services will become available to the travelling public

In the meantime, this shortage may affect YOUR train

TO RESTORE PRE-WAR STANDARDS WILL TAKE TIME

GWR · LMS · LNER · SR

The above series of adverts appeared in *The Kidderminster Shuttle* during 1946.

The above series of adverts appeared in *The Kidderminster Shuttle* in late 1946

The 1947 winter snow disruptions

The severe winter at the beginning of 1947 caused widespread disruption on the railways. The Kidderminster area was also affected and the following observations were made during this period :

9 February 1947

0-6-0T 2712 (STB) fitted with a large snowplough was noted going down the branch towards Bewdley.

5 March 1947

The train from Cardiff due at Kidderminster at 8.13 p.m was reported to have arrived at about 3.30 a.m.

6 March 1947

The Shrewsbury to Hereford line blocked by snow. Trains diverted via Kidderminster. 6963 *Throwley Hall* (SALOP) was noted on a Manchester to Penzance train. 5045 *Earl of Dudley* (PDN) was also noted.

7 March 1947

3273 *Mounts Bay* (SALOP), 3377 (SALOP), 4114 (WOS), 4546 (WOS), 4584 (CHEL), 4107 (TYS), 4641 (WOS) and 6353 (CDF) all noted as working from Kidderminster shed.

9 March 1947

The train from Cardiff due at Kidderminster at 11.10 a.m arrived 80 minutes late.

10 March 1947

6804 *Brockington Grange* (WES) was on the 6.19 p.m train to Malvern Wells, normally a KDR turn.

Other disruptions in 1947 -1949

6 September 1947

Railcar 7 derailed on station crossover. Single line working 6.0 a.m until 9.30 a.m. Worcester breakdown train headed by 4504 (WOS)

8 October 1947

Shrewsbury to Hereford line blocked. Trains diverted via Kidderminster.
5082 *Swordfish* (BL) noted on a train from Hereford.

30 December 1948

Kidderminster to Shrewsbury line blocked at Arley due to landslide.

15 January 1949

Railcar 32 failed. Replaced by 2-6-0 6382 (KDR) with 2 coaches on Tenbury services.

WHY NATIONALISE
TRANSPORT ?

○ The Government propose to introduce a Bill to nationalise transport.

● The Railways and the Road Hauliers have submitted a plan to the Government which, while securing the co-ordination of freight transport, would leave the traders and the public with complete freedom to use any form of transport including their own.

● As stated by the Lord President of the Council : "LET THE ARGUMENT BE DIRECTED TO THE MERITS AND LET THE TEST BE THE PUBLIC INTEREST."

● The Public are asked to support the demand for an enquiry before being committed to any scheme which might damage irretrievably the country's industrial prosperity.

GWR · LMS · LNER · SR
ROAD HAULAGE ASSOCIATION

The Great Western Railway ceased to exist becoming British Railways (Western Region) on 1 January 1948.

In the transition period before the British Railways renumbering system had been decided upon GWR locomotives entering works had a small 'W' painted below the cabside number plates. This was soon painted out when it had been decided that ex GWR locomotives would retain their numbers.

On 2 February 1948 2-6-2T 4100 (KDR) was the first to be noted painted unlined black with 'BRITISH RAILWAYS' on the tanks in GWR style lettering and with the 'W' beneath the number plates.

In the first few months after Nationalisation various liveries were to be seen :

Black, lined and unlined, with lettering.

Black, lined and unlined, without any lettering.

Green, lined and unlined, with lettering.

Green, lined and unlined, without lettering.

Light Green, lined with lettering.

A few recorded observations:

3 July 1948   7010 *Avondale Castle* (OXF) Experimental light green, red/cream/grey lining, GW style lettering in white on tender, brass smoke box number.

12 October 1948   5156 (TYS)   Black, lined red/cream/grey, no lettering, smoke box number plate.

1 November 1948   4128 (BHD) Black, unlined, no lettering, smoke box number plate.

8 November 1948   6916 *Misterton Hall* (WOS) Black, red/cream/grey lining, smoke box number plate

Cast Iron smokebox number plates began to appear in September 1948 replacing the painted buffer beam numbers. Lion and Wheel emblems incorporating the words 'BRITISH RAILWAYS' also began to appear about this time.

KIDDERMINSTER LOCO DEPOT

KDR

ALLOCATION JANUARY 1940

5112	2-6-2T	5114	2-6-2T	8101	2-6-2T	4586	2-6-2T	4594	2-6-2T
4596	2-6-2T	5518	2-6-2T	5573	2-6-2T	4845	0-4-2T *	6430	0-6-0T *
7741	0-6-0T	8718	0-6-0T	8727	0-6-0T	28	0-6-0T CMDP	29	0-6-0T CMDP

*Auto fitted

Total 15

ALLOCATION JANUARY 1945

5110	2-6-2T	5112	2-6-2T	8101	2-6-2T	4586	2-6-2T	4594	2-6-2T
4596	2-6-2T	5518	2-6-2T	5573	2-6-2T	4625	0-6-0T	7700	0-6-0T
8718	0-6-0T	8727	0-6-0T	2044	0-6-0T	28	0-6-0T CMDP	29	0-6-0T CMDP

LNER 1986 Class J.25 0-6-0	LNER 1989 Class J.25 0-6-0	LNER 1994 Class J.25 0-6-0
LNER 2040 Class J.25 0-6-0	LNER 2051 Class J.25 0-6-0	LNER 2053 Class J.25 0-6-0
LNER 2134 Class J.25 0-6-0	LNER 2138 Class J.25 0-6-0	

Total 23

Railcars 5 and 6 stored.

ALLOCATION JANUARY 1948

4100	2-6-2T	4153	2-6-2T	5110	2-6-2T	8101	2-6-2T	4584	2-6-2T
4586	2-6-2T	4594	2-6-2T	5518	2-6-2T	5573	2-6-2T	5303	2-6-0
4625	0-6-0T	4641	0-6-0T	7700	0-6-0T	8718	0-6-0T	8727	0-6-0T
2093	0-6-0T	28	0-6-0T CMDP	29	0-6-0T CMDP				

Total 18

ALLOCATION DECEMBER 1949

4100	2-6-2T	4153	2-6-2T	4175	2-6-2T	5110	2-6-2T	8101	2-6-2T
4518	2-6-2T	4586	2-6-2T	4594	2-6-2T	4599	2-6-2T	5518	2-6-2T
6382	2-6-0	3601	0-6-0T	4625	0-6-0T	7700	0-6-0T	8718	0-6-0T
8727	0-6-0T	2051	0-6-0T	28	0-6-0T CMDP	29	0-6-0T CMDP		

Total 19

National Railway Museum

National Railway Museum

Official photographs taken shortly after the opening of the shed in 1932.

National Railway Museum

Locos in shed 2-4-0T, 0-4-2T, 57XX 0-6-0T and 45XX 2-6-2T

National Railway Museum

Official photographs taken shortly after the opening in 1932

J.Davenport / Initial Photographics

2-6-2T 8101 arrived at Kidderminster new in 1938 and remained until its withdrawal in 1961

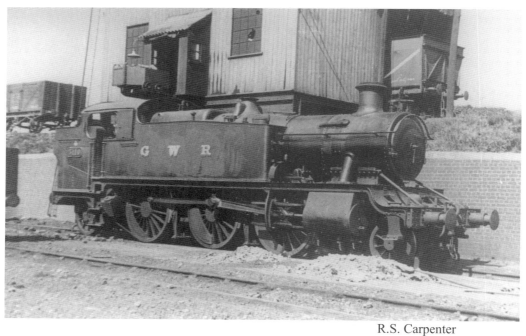

R.S. Carpenter

2-6-2T 5110   in 1947
A Kidderminster engine from 1940 until 1958

J.Davenport /Initial Photographics

2-6-2T 5518 spent most of its life at Kidderminster between 1938 and 1960

J.Davenport / Initial Photographics

2-6-2T 4594 a Kidderminster engine from 1934 to 1952

B.K.B Green / Initial Photographics

2-6-2T 4596

Came to Kidderminster in 1932 staying until 1945, it returned in 1951 remaining until 1957.

J.Davenport / Initial Photographics

3601 was transferred to Kidderminster from Hereford in September 1949 initially to work the Tenbury goods, it remained at Kidderminster until the closure of the shed in August 1964. 5394 arrived in January 1955 and remained until its withdrawal in 1959.

J.Davenport / Initial Photographics

0-6-0T 7700 a Kidderminster engine from 1944 until its withdrawal in 1961.

Peter F Curtis.

0-6-2T 6617 and 0-6-0T 7750, both on loan to Kidderminster
2 March 1947

F.A Wycherley

0-6-0T 4625 brand new to Kidderminster in September 1942
Remained until 1953

Author's collection

0-6-0T 8718 was a Kidderminster engine for 30 years
1934 – 1964

A.J Turley

Collett 0-6-0 2281
Transferred to Kidderminster in 1948 for working the Tenbury goods.

A. Norman H. Glover

2-6-0 Mogul 6382 in shed yard in 1949
A regular on the Alveley coal trains

H.F Wheeler

3393 *Australia* at Swindon

Bulldog 4-4-0 3393 *Australia* was the only named engine to be officially allocated to Kidderminster. It arrived in January 1946 and was mainly used on goods trains to Shrewsbury before departing in July 1946.

Peter F Curtis

1206 in Kidderminster yard May 1947

Probably the most unusual locomotive to be allocated to Kidderminster was Alexandra Dock Railway 2-6-2T No. 1206 which was transferred from Newport Pill in April 1947. It was mainly used in the goods yard and on trips to Foley Park until it was transferred to Hereford in October 1947.

126

2021 Class 0-6-0T 2051
A Kidderminster engine from 1948 until its withdrawal in 1952.

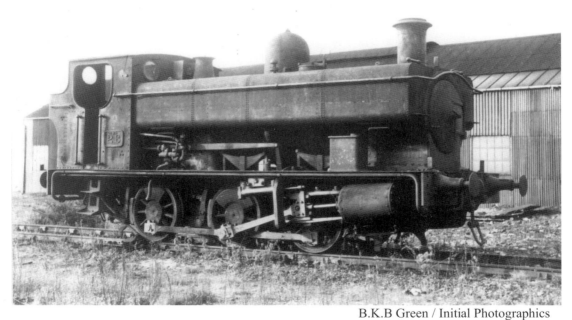

CMDP 0-6-0T 28
Stored in 1948 with spark arrester removed.

A. Norman Glover

CMDP 0-6-0T 29
The CMDP locomotives were fitted with spark arresters for working ammunition trains
from Cleobury Mortimer to the Naval Depot at Ditton Priors.

V.R Webster

LNER Class J.25 0-6-0 No. 2134
14 March 1945

V.R Webster

LNER Class J.25 0-6-0 Nos. 2053 and 1986
Kidderminster MPD   14 March 1945

Visiting Locomotives

On most Sundays between March and May 1945, when alterations were being made to the coaling facilities at Worcester, several locomotives were sent to Kidderminster shed for servicing. The following were noted during this period:

Sunday 18 March 1945 … 4906 *Bradfield Hall* (TR), 7200 (LLY), 7214 (CDF), 3043 (SRD), *6632* (PT)

Sunday 25 March 1945 … 7806 *Cockington Manor* (BAN), 2955 *Tortworth Court* (BL), 2829 (STJ), LMS 8427 (OXY), LMS 8460 (OXY).

Sunday 1 April 1945 …… 8393 (BHD), LMS 8428 (OXY), 3833 (NPT), 5360 (SHL), 3382 (WOS), 4285 (ABDR), 4004 *Morning Star* (OXF), 3037 (PPRD), 2897 (CDF), 5921 *Bingley Hall* (OXY), 4924 *Eydon Hall*.

Sunday 8 April 1945 …… 2881 (PDN), 2845 (SHL), 5388 (CDF), 6936 (un-named) (WOS), 5228 (LLY), LMS 8406 (DID), LMS 8408 (NA).

Sunday 15 April 1945 ….   5331 (OXY), LMS 8467 (STJ), 3812 (STJ), 4903 *Astley Hall* (OXF), 2292 (BAN), 3406 *Calcutta* (NPT), 6921 (un-named) (WOS).

Sunday 22 April 1945 …. 3353 *Pershore Plum* (WOS), 2277 (WOS), 3802 (BAN), 2833 (BAN), LMS 8430 (OXY), 6374 (SDN).

Sunday 6 May 1945 ……. 4000 *North Star* (SRD), 6846 *Ruckley Grange* (BL), 4265 (SED), 7203 (NPT) 6926 (un-named) (NPT)

Sunday 20 May 1945 ....   7802 *Bradley Manor* (SPM), 3418 *Sir Arthur Yorke* (RDG), LMS 8408 (NA), 6970 (un-named) (OXY), LMS 8462 (NPT), 2612 (BAN), 3848 (OXF).

Sunday 27 May 1945 ....   2936 *Cefntilla Court* (CDF), 2955 *Tortworth Court* (BL), 5346 (TYS), 5386 (OXY), 2827 (PDN), 2858 (SHL).

Peter F. Curtis

0-6-0 Saddle tank 2007 (WOS)
Stored on the 'dump' awaiting works. March 1947

Locomotives awaiting works were often sent from Worcester to Kidderminster shed for storage until a space became available at Swindon Works.

5000 *Launceston Castle* (PDN) was stopped at Kidderminster on 11 March 1944 and remained on shed until 3 April 1944 when it was sent to Swindon.

Locomotives sent from Worcester awaiting works included :
7818 *Granville Manor* (WOS)	21 March 1944 – 11 April 1944
5063 *Earl Baldwin* (WOS)	30 May 1944 - 7 June 1944, 19 May 1945 – 30 August 1945
5017 *St. Donats Castle* (SRD)	1 November 1945
4092 *Dunraven Castle* (WOS)	1 February 1946 – 19 February 1946
4975 *Umberslade Hall* (CDF)	23 March 1946 – 5 April 1946
6938 un-named (WOS)	17 January 1946 – 18 February 1946
LMS 8442 (PDN)	- 5 January 1945
LMS 8452 (GLO)	21 May 1946 – 30 June 1946
3030 (WOS)	2 January 1946 – 19 February 1946
3022 (SPM)	24 July 1947 – 27 August 1947
3048 (WOS)	29 March 1947 – 4 July 1947

Kidderminster Loco Shed Visits (Unofficial !)

On Sunday afternoons the shed was usually unattended so the opportunity was frequently taken to discover what locomotives were hidden in the shed.

Sunday 15 July 1945 the following were on shed :
CMDP 0-6-0T   28 (KDR) with spark arrester
2-6-2T   4534 (HFD) on loan, 4586 (KDR), 5518 (KDR), 5573 (KDR), 8101 (KDR)
0-6-0T   2044 (KDR) with spark arrester, 7700 (KDR), 4625 (KDR), 4659 (HFD) under repair,
               8727 (KDR)
0-6-0   2234 (SALOP)
LNER Class J.25 0-6-0   1986 (KDR), 1989 (KDR), 2053 (KDR), 2134 (KDR), 2136 (KDR, 2142 (KDR)

4-6-0 5063 *Earl Baldwin* (WOS) stored awaiting works.
Railcar No. 5 stored.

Sunday 23 June 1946 the following were on shed :
CMDP 0-6-0T   29 (KDR) with spark arrester
2-6-2T   4546 (WOS) on loan, 4586 (KDR), 4594 (KDR), 5518 (KDR), 5110 (KDR), 5190 (TYS),
               8101 (KDR)
0-6-0T   2044 (KDR) with spark arrester, 4629 (KDR), 8718 (KDR), 8727 (KDR)
4-4-0   3273 *Mounts Bay* (SALOP)
2-6-0   5303 (KDR)
LNER Class J.25 0-6-0   2136 (KDR), 2138 (KDR), 5704 (KDR) renumbered from 2051

2-8-0   3021 (HFD) stored awaiting works.

Sunday 2 March 1947 the following were on shed :
CMDP 0-6-0T   29 (KDR) with spark arrester
2-6-2T   4584 (CHEL) on loan, 4586 (KDR), 4594(KDR), 5518 (KDR), 5573 (KDR)
0-6-0T   2093 (KDR) with spark arrester, 3615 (SRD) on loan, 7700 (KDR), 7750 (WOS) on loan,
               8718 (KDR), 8727 (KDR)
0-6-2T   6617 (STB)
2-6-0   6353 (CDF) on loan
0-6-0   2228 (SALOP)

0-6-0ST   2007 (WOS) stored awaiting works.

BRITISH RAILWAYS ROUTE KNOWLEDGE CARD

B.R. 32707/5

Depot: KIDDERMINSTER

Name .... No. ....

(in Block Letters)

Grade ....

Section of Line	Certification		Cancellation	
	Initials	Date	Initials	Date
Worcester & Paddn. P. via Honeybourne				
Worcester & Reading P & W. Jcn.				
Paddington & O.O. Common Shed				
Worcester & Oxford P. Station				
Worcester & Oxford Hinksey Sidings				
Worcester & Kingham				
Worcester & Honeybourne				
Worcester & Moreton-in-Marsh				
Worcester & Evesham				
Honeybourne & Leamington				
Leamington & Banbury Shed				
Kingham & Banbury				
Honeybourne & Stratford-on-Avon				
Stratford-on-Avon & Tyseley via Earlswood Lakes				
Stratford-on-Avon & Tyseley via Hatton				
Tyseley & Birmingham Snow Hill				
Worcester & Lapworth via Stourbridge				
Worcester & Birmingham Snow Hill via Stourbridge				
Worcester & Stourbridge Jcn.				
Worcester & Kidderminster				
Stourbridge Jcn. & Crewe via Oxley				
Stourbridge Jcn. & Crewe via Wombourn				
Stourbridge Jcn. & Oxley Sidings via Dudley				
Stourbridge Jcn. & Oxley Sidings via Wombourn				
Stourbridge Jcn. & Dudley				
Worcester & Birmingham New St.				
Worcester & Stoke Wks.				
Worcester & Bewdley via Hartlebury				
Worcester & Bewdley via Kidderminster				
Bewdley & Crewe via Salop				
Bewdley & Shrewsbury				
Bewdley & Ironbridge & Broseley				
Bewdley & Bridgnorth				
Bewdley & Cleobury Mortimer & Tenbury Wells				
Worcester & Bromyard				
Worcester & Hereford Barrs Court				
Worcester & Hereford Barton				
Worcester & Malvern				
Worcester & Colwall				

132

Worcester & Ledbury				
Leominster & Bewdley				
Leominster & Tenbury Wells				
Woofferton and Kidderminster				
Leominster & Kington				
Worcester Shed & Worcester Shrub Hill				
Worcester Shed & Worcester Foregate St.				
Worcester Shed & all Local Shunting Yards				
Kidderminster & Stourport via Hartlebury				
Kidderminster & Stourport via Bewdley				
Kidderminster Shed & Shunting Yards				
Kidderminster Shed & M.E.B. Power Station				
Kidderminster and Birmingham via Great Bridge				
Birmingham and Wolverhampton Main Line				

Route Knowledge Card for Kidderminster Shed
probably dating from late 1940s or early 1950s

Instructions for Working of Engines to and from Kidderminster Shed.
Service Timetable Appendix dated February 1943.

Working of Engines to and from the Engine Shed Sidings, Kidderminster.

Engines proceeding to or from the engine shed pass through the connection from the Bewdley Branch and Down Goods Running Loop lines.

The loop lines immediately inside the Down Goods Loop connection are used as ingoing and outgoing running roads respectively ; one way spring points being provided at each end of the loop lines, normally set to divert engines to the left-hand side when travelling in either direction.

When an engine is ready to enter the Sidings, the Signalman at Kidderminster Junction, if he is in a position to do so, will set the points for the Engine Shed, but the Driver must not regard this as an indication that the line is clear, and he will be responsible for stopping short of any obstruction.

A treadle is fixed on the ingoing loop line 70 yards in advance of the catch point ; the operation of the treadle sets in motion a buzzer in Kidderminster Junction Signal Box as an indication to the Signalman that an engine or engines coupled have passed inside clear of the Engine Shed Siding points.

An engine leaving the shed for the Main line may proceed as far as the signal controlling the exit from the Engine Shed Siding, at which point it must be brought to a stand ; the Fireman must then proceed to the telephone (fixed near the spot) and advise the Signalman the engine is ready to leave and to what point it is proceeding ; if an engine is detained at this signal the Fireman must immediately proceed to the telephone on hearing the bell ring , outgoing engines must be given priority over engines proceeding to shed.

Should an engine be required to run from the engine shed Sidings to the Station through the Goods Yard, the Signalman will so advise the Fireman who makes the telephone enquiry.

Working to and from Kidderminster Engine Shed (and Sand) Sidings.

An engine and wagons, or set of coaches, must not be allowed to leave the Goods Yard for the engine shed or Sand Sidings until the Yard Foreman has obtained authority for the movement from the locomotive shed Foreman over the telephone. A train of coaches from the Main line for the Siding must not be allowed to proceed to the Siding until the Signalman has obtained authority for the movement from the locomotive shed Foreman. After giving authority for the movement the locomotive shed Foreman must see that any connection over which the engine with wagons or set of coaches will run is not fouled.

An engine with wagons from the Goods Yard for the engine shed or Sand Sidings may propel into the sidings but the Shunter must precede the movement on foot in order to establish the line over which the operation is being made inside the Engine Shed Sidings is clear.

When an engine propels vehicles into the engine shed Siding the buzzer referred to in the previous instructions will be set in motion before the whole of the vehicles are clear inside the loop ; the Shunter in charge of the movement must, therefore, advise the Junction Signalman by telephone when the vehicles and engine are inside clear ; the Signalman must not reverse the points leading to the engine shed Sidings until he has received this advice from the Shunter.

H. Whitehouse's Sand Siding between Kidderminster and Bewdley at 135 miles 60 chains.

This Siding (holding capacity, 12 wagons) is situated on the single line between Kidderminster Junction and Bewdley South on a gradient of 1 in 112, falling towards Bewdley. The points leading to the Siding are facing to trains from the direction of Bewdley, and are worked from a ground frame locked by the Electric Train Token for the Kidderminster Junction—Bewdley South Section.

Traffic from and to the Siding will be worked from Kidderminster Yard by the Kidderminster shunting engine, being signalled under Electric Train Token Regulation 13, Clause (a), at agreed times or according to circumstances. When loaded wagons are to be worked from the Siding, the engine and van must go to the Siding for this purpose, the brake van must be left (properly secured) on the running line while the traffic is picked up, and after this has been done, the train must be propelled back to Kidderminster Junction. Empty vehicles for the Siding must be drawn to the Siding and after being detached in the Siding the engine must propel the brake van back to Kidderminster Junction.

Before movements into the Siding are commenced, the gate must be opened, effectively secured to the post provided, and the wheel stop removed from the rail ; care must be taken to safely secure all vehicles left in the Siding replace the wheel stop and close the gate after each operation is completed.

A gantry and sand mill exist across the Siding at a point approximately 50 yards inside the gate.

This structure will provide clearance of 9 ft. 0 in. only above rail level and vans or open wagons of more than 7 planks in height (8 planks in case of S.R. wagons) are prohibited from working into the Private Siding.

A Guard or Shunter must accompany each trip and ride in the brake van. During the propelling movement the Guard or Shunter must keep a sharp lookout, and be prepared to exhibit to the Driver any necessary hand signal; trips returning to the Goods Yard must be dealt with in accordance with the instructions governing " admittance of Freight trains direct from the branch line to the front siding, Kidderminster Junction," with the exception that they must be brought to a stand at Kidderminster Junction Down branch home signal. If this signal is not immediately lowered, the Guard or Shunter in charge must proceed to the telephone in the vicinity and advise the Junction Box Signalman the trip is waiting to enter the Yard.

A white light must be carried on the brake van during the propelling movement after sunset, facing in the direction of Kidderminster Junction. The engine must carry a lamp shewing a red light to the rear during the propelling movement.

The propelling movements may take place in clear weather only. Driver to proceed cautiously at reduced speed and keep a sharp lookout for hand signals.

Under no circumstances must vehicles, other than the brake van which must always have the hand brake screwed on tightly before it is detached from the train, be allowed to stand on the Main line unless the engine is coupled to the vehicles.

Instructions for train working to Whitehouse's siding.
Service Timetable Appendix dated February 1943.

HOOBROOK VIADUCT

Hoobrook Viaduct is the largest railway structure in Kidderminster. Opened in 1885 it replaced an earlier wooden viaduct. Having 20 arches and containing seven million bricks it is a most impressive structure.

LOCAL GOODS BRAKE VANS

During the early years of the war brake vans were pooled and the names of their home depot was deleted. This was to avoid unnecessary working back to their depot when used on unbalanced turns.

Towards the end of the 1940s the GWR practice of branding vans with their home depot was resumed with their workings. R.U = Restricted Use. 1949 brandings of local vans are shown below. They were all 20 ton except for 6 wheel van 56963 which was 24 tons.

56684 KIDDERMINSTER RU
11.30 am Kidderminster to Woofferton
4.0 pm Woofferton to Kidderminster

68632 KIDDERMINSTER RU
Trips to Foley Park

114982 KIDDERMINSTER RU
Trips to Foley Park

56512 and 35970 HARTLEBURY RU
9.30 am Hartlebury to Shrewsbury
8.20 am Shrewsbury to Kidderminster
10.5 pm Kidderminster to Hartlebury (Light)

11478 KIDDERMINSTER RU
9.55 am Kidderminster to Alveley
Alveley to Buildwas
(SO) Stourport on return
2.0 pm (SX) Alveley to Kidderminster
2.30 pm (SO) Stourport to Worcester
5.10 pm (SO) Worcester to Kidderminster

56644 and 68763 HARTLEBURY RU
5.45 am Hartlebury to Alveley
10.45 am Alveley to Hartlebury
2.15 pm Hartlebury to Shrewsbury (SX)
11.30 am Shrewsbury to Hartlebury (SX)

17833 and 56963 HARTLEBURY RU
(no workings on these , but were used on the Stourport slack trips.)

A.J. Turley

A rare photograph of Kidderminster Brake Vans 11478 and 56684

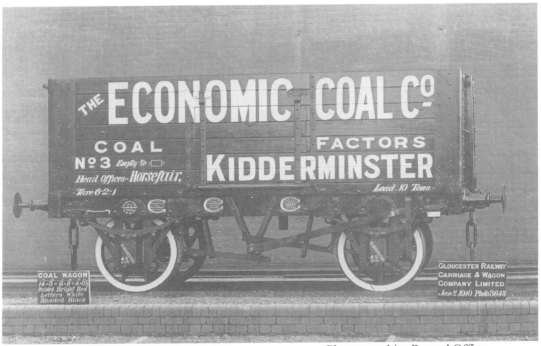

Several of the local coal merchants had their own wagons.

Harry Whitehouse had three sand quarries, one at Wilden, near Stourport and two at Kidderminster, one being near the bottom goods yard and one on the opposite side of the Bewdley line to the engine shed.

The Railway Carriers

The local carriers for the railway were Messrs Thomas Bantock & Co., Agents for the GWR, with their offices and stables in Marlborough Street and the L.M.S.R, who, although not having a passenger station, had their own goods depot and stables in Oxford Street.

Horse power was still much in evidence during the 1940s. Every weekday they could be seen hauling drays loaded up with carpets up Station Hill towards the railway station.

Kidderminster Library
Thomas Bantock & Co. stables in Marlborough Street, Kidderminster.

137

London, Midland & Scottish Railway

National Railway Museum

L.M.S.R offices and stables in Oxford Street, Kidderminster.

Brintons Limited

L.M.S.R Wharf and canal side warehouse near St. Mary's church.

Robert Barber

A horse and dray being loaded at a local carpet factory

National Railway Museum

Thomas Bantock & Co. horse at work at Kidderminster Goods Depot.

Railway horses and their handlers line up for a photograph, possibly a May Day occasion in the late 1920s. The Worcester Cross Hotel is in the background.

On 1 July 1860 the Oxford, Worcester and Wolverhampton Railway became the West Midland Railway. This was, however to be short lived when on 1 August 1863 it became part of the Great Western Railway. A public house named after the West Midland Railway was situated in Worcester Street, near the bottom of Station Hill. This was closed in October 1968 to make way for the ring road.

APPENDIX

Summary of GWR Locomotive Classes
Observed by the Author at Kidderminster 1940 – 1949

Class		Loco number series	Number of locos In service	Number seen at Kidderminster
4-6-0	Castle	40XX, 50XX, 70XX	161	153
	County	10XX	30	23
	Star	40XX	48	48
	Saint	29XX	54	53
	Hall	49XX, 59XX, 69XX, 79XX	306	296
	Grange	68XX	80	79
	Manor	78XX	20	20
4-4-0	Duke	32XX (90XX)	11	11
	Dukedog	32XX (90XX)	29	21
	Bulldog	33XX, 34XX	55	35
2-8-0	Consolidation	28XX, 38XX	167	167
		47XX	9	3
	R.O.D	30XX	50	50
2-6-0	Mogul	43XX, 53XX, 63XX, 73XX, 83XX	222	219
		93XX	20	20
	Aberdare	26XX	32	32
0-6-0	Dean	23XX, 24XX, 25XX	122	32
	Dean (Double frame)	23XX	3	3
	Collett	22XX	120	64
2-8-2T		72XX	54	54
2-8-0T		42XX, 52XX	151	146
2-6-2T		31XX	5	5
	3150	31XX	36	13
	Prairie	41XX, 51XX	170	117
		61XX	70	2
		81XX	10	8
	Small Prairie	45XX, 55XX	175	29
0-6-2T		56XX, 66XX	200	88

The numerous 0-6-0T and 0-4-2T and 2-4-0T classes are not included in this list. The local ones from the Worcester and Wolverhampton Divisions were common, but those from distant sheds were rarely seen.

No 4-6-0 King Class locomotives came through as they were prohibited.

No 44XX 2-6-2T locomotives were observed during this period.

GWR SHED CODES

LONDON DIVISION

DID ...... Didcot	PDN ...... Paddington	OXF ...... Oxford
RDG ...... Reading	SHL ...... Southall	SLO ...... Slough

BRISTOL DIVISION

BL ...... Bristol, Bath Road	SPM ...... Bristol St. Philips Marsh	
SDN ...... Swindon	WEY ...... Weymouth	WES ...... Westbury
YEO ...... Yeovil		

NEWTON ABBOT DIVISION

EXE ...... Exeter	LA ...... Laira	NA ...... Newton Abbot
PZ ...... Penzance	STBZ ..... St. Blazey	TN ...... Taunton
TR ...... Truro		

WOLVERHAMPTON DIVISION

BAN ...... Banbury	BHD ...... Birkenhead	CHR ...... Chester
CNYD .... Croes Newydd	LMTN .... Leamington	OXY ...... Oxley
SALOP .... Shrewsbury	STB ...... Stourbridge	TYS .... Tyseley
WLN ...... Wellington	SRD ...... Wolverhampton, Stafford Road	

WORCESTER DIVISION

CHEL ..... Cheltenham	GLO ...... Gloucester	HFD ...... Hereford
KDR ...... Kidderminster	LYD ...... Lydney	WOS ......Worcester

NEWPORT DIVISION

ABG ...... Aberbeeg	ABDR ......Aberdare	CDF ...... Cardiff, Canton
NPT .... Newport Ebbw	LTS ....Llantrisant	PILL ...... Newport Pill
PPRD ...... Pontypool Road	STJ ...... Severn Tunnel Jc	TDU ...... Tondu.

NEATH DIVISION

BP .... Burry Port	CARM ...... Carmarthen	DG .... Danygraig
FGD .... Fishguard	LDR .... Landore	LLY ...... Llanelly
NEA .... Neath	NEY .... Neyland	PFFN .... Pantyffynnon
PT .... Port Talbot	SED ......Swansea East Dock	WTD ..... Whitland

CARDIFF VALLEYS DIVISION

AYN .... Abercynon	BRY .... Barry	CH .... Caeharris
CYS .... Cardiff Cathays	DC .... Dowlais Central	FDL ...... Ferndale
MTHR ... Merthyr	RYR .... Radyr	RHY ...... Rhymney
TRE .... Treherbert		

CENTRAL WALES DIVISION

ABH .... Aberystwyth	BCN .... Brecon	MCH ......Machynlleth
OSW .... Oswestry		